Ann Judson:
a missionary life for Burma

Sharon James

EP BOOKS

1st Floor Venture House, 6 Silver Court, Watchmead, Welwyn Garden City, UK, AL7 1TS

e-mail: sales@epbooks.org

EP books are distributed in the USA by:

JPL Fulfillment

3741 Linden Avenue Southeast,

Grand Rapids, MI 49548

orders@jplbooks.com

Tel: 877.683.6935

First published 1998 as *My Heart in His Hands*

Second impression 2000

Third impression 2003

Fourth impression 2006

Fifth impression 2010

Sixth impression 2012

This edition 2017

British Library Cataloguing in Publication Data available

ISBN: 978–0–85234–916–8

To Bill

Ann Judson

Contents

List of illustrations and maps

Foreword

In the summer of 2005 our oldest son and his wife and family left Surrey for Massachusetts, New England. For four years they lived in South Hamilton. At the end of their third year they were joined by our daughter, her husband and children. So for six years, Pauline and I made annual trips to one of the most beautiful parts of the world. We fell in love with New England not least because of its association with three of our Christian heroes: George Whitefield (whose bones are interred in Newburyport) and Ann and Adoniram Judson. It was a five minute drive from the Gordon Conwell Seminary campus to Wenham where Adoniram spent seven years as a child living in the parsonage.

Not much further away, in Haverhill, where our children took their USA driving tests, Ann Judson was born. Five miles South of Wenham is the seaside town of Salem from where the Judsons sailed to take the Good News of the Gospel to the Buddhist communities of Burma.

I first read Sharon James' biography of Ann Judson before our trips to New England began. My subsequent readings have been enriched

by the first hand associations I can now make with the area in which the Judsons grew up, fell in love, married, and departed as missionaries.

Sharon has given us a tremendously moving account of Ann Judson's thirty-seven years. She has skilfully and seamlessly woven her own narrative with Ann's personal correspondence and has vividly captured the times in which her subjects lived. I found myself living within their story.

The greatest impact of the book is made by its description of Ann Judson's passion for the glory of God and her single-minded desire to see the kingdom of Jesus Christ established in Burma. The faith and endurance of this woman are, at times, breath-taking. In particular, the chapters that deal with Ann's response to her husband's imprisonment are both harrowing and inspiring. What she accomplished for her husband's welfare whilst suffering poor health and carrying a babe-in-arms is nothing short of astonishing.

Over the last ten years there have been times in my own ministry when I have felt like slipping quietly into a comfortable retirement. But, I have been motivated to persevere in pastoral work not least by this book and by its portrayal of the persevering faith of the godly and beautiful Ann.

I would commend this book to both men and women who want to grow in faith and godliness.

John Tindall
Birmingham

Introduction

I initially completed a biography of Ann Judson (*My Heart in His Hands*) in 1998 because I had myself been deeply challenged by her life. Since then, I have been delighted to hear from many who have read her story, and been inspired to greater commitment to world mission.

As this new edition of Ann Judson's life is published, my desire is that it would stir up concern for the people of Burma. I also hope that the example of Ann Judson's willingness to give her life for the cause of the Gospel will inspire concern for the many people groups in the world who, as yet, have not heard the Gospel. It is estimated that at least a third of the world's population is unreached. If Ann and Adoniram Judson were alive today, I am certain that they would urge Christians to use *Operation World* (7th edition, 2010, WEC/Biblica), praying that the Gospel would be 'preached in the whole world as a testimony to all nations' (Matthew 24:14).

Sharon James,
Leamington Spa, 2015.

Introduction to the 1998 edition,
My Heart in His Hands

The *Memoir of Mrs Judson*, written by James Knowles and published in 1829 became one of the classic missionary biographies of the nineteenth century. It was referred to by one as "a book so universally known that it scarcely need be mentioned."[1] As one of the first female American missionaries,[2] Ann Judson worked alongside her husband in evangelism, she was active in teaching, her translation and writing output was formidable. Perhaps her influence was greatest as a publicist for the newly inaugurated mission movement. Her book, *An Account of the American Baptist Mission to the Burman Empire* was published in 1823 and widely read in both America and Britain.

Ann's life was relatively short. She was born in New England in 1789. In 1812 she married Adoniram Judson and sailed for India. They settled in Burma in 1813, and thirteen years later, in 1826, she died, aged 37. For the previous two years no-one had known whether they were alive or dead. They had been trapped in the capital of Burma when the first Anglo-Burman war broke out in 1824. When the true

story of Adoniram's horrific imprisonment and Ann's fearless efforts on his behalf became known, their fame was ensured. At that time, (before sports heroes, rock stars and super models) heroic pioneer missionaries, especially if they died early, assumed celebrity status. When the *Memoir* appeared shortly after Ann's death, she was virtually canonised by the American Protestant public.

The *Memoir* has been out of print for many years. Knowles based his work on what remained of Ann's own diary and letters, he incorporated large sections of her book, and used other primary sources such as letters from her husband.[3] The length would deter many modern readers; moreover the conventions of the time dictated a writing style very different to today. Rather than paraphrase the entire *Memoir*, many of the most significant sections have been reprinted as they appeared in the original, with minimal editorial amendment. This preserves their value as a primary source for the life of the Judsons, as well as giving an authentic flavour of the piety of the time. Page references to the 1829 edition of the *Memoir* are provided after each quotation or extract.

A narrative is provided to link these original sections of the *Memoir*. Where other sources are used these have been footnoted. During his last years Adoniram shared many early memories with his third wife, Emily. She had been a well-known literary figure before her marriage to Judson, and was able to record many of his reminiscences in a distinctively vivid style. She supplied much material to Frances Wayland, appointed by the Mission Board as Adoniram's official biographer. Judson's son Edward also wrote a comprehensive biography of his father. In addition to these sources I have drawn on some unpublished letters, and Ann's book *An Account of the American Baptist Mission*.

To contemporary readers the tone of several of the extracts may sound patronising, and even racist. But it should be remembered that the Judsons were children of their time. In all fairness Adoniram's mission policy was to train national workers as fast as possible (a strategy that was ahead of his time). We would, today, love to know far more about the Burmese Christians who appear in the story; especially the faithful Moung Ing who stood alongside the Judsons in the darkest days.[4] But those who wrote the memoirs of Ann and Adoniram were not writing for a post-colonial audience. (It should be understood that when Ann referred to "heathen" or "natives" that this reflected common use of language at the time; the modern reader should understand "non-Christian" or "locals" where these terms are used).

Ann's friends and family sometimes affectionately called her "Nancy" (this is the name used throughout Courtney Anderson's classic work *To the Golden Shore*). But in all the correspondence and other writings I have referred to the name "Ann" is used, and so for the sake of consistency this name has been used throughout.

I am grateful to the Evangelical Library, London, and to Mrs Susan Mills of the Angus Library, Oxford, for help in locating sources, and to all the staff at EP for their patience and help. Thanks are due to all those who have read all or part of the manuscript, and to those who have given encouragement to persevere with this project, especially David Clark and Michael Haykin. Throughout the time of writing I have been thankful to be part of the church family at Emmanuel. Most of all thanks are due to Bill, for without his help this book would never have been contemplated, let alone completed.

Sharon James,
Leamington Spa, 1998.

'One of the happiest creatures on earth' (1789–1806)

If you had visited the quiet New England town of Bradford at the turn of the nineteenth century, you could not have missed the Hasseltine household. On summer evenings lights would blaze and music would sound out until late into the night. The generous and affable John Hasseltine had built a room in his spacious home in which to hold parties for his five youngsters and their friends. John and Rebecca were hospitable and, with four eligible daughters, their home was a social centre of the town. Like most families in Bradford, they attended the Congregational Church which stood at the centre of the community—geographically and psychologically. But religion was fairly undemanding; the main business of life was enjoyment.

Ann, sometimes known affectionately as 'Nancy', was born just before Christmas in 1789. The youngest of John and Rebecca's five children, she was doted on by the family, and an especial favourite of

her warm-hearted father. Lively, adventurous, cheerful, determined, highly intelligent—she was not in the least overshadowed by John, Rebecca, Abigail and Mary. She had a wonderfully happy childhood, and by her early teens she was sparkling, popular and very attractive, always in demand for parties and other social events. As one friend said, 'Where Ann is, no one could be gloomy or unhappy.' She maintained a pattern of prayer and dutifully attended church, but despite considerable academic promise her main concerns were friends and socializing. Ann confided in her diary that she often thought herself 'one of the happiest creatures on earth'.

And then, in May 1805, a new teacher arrived at Bradford Academy. He was intensely serious. He believed in heaven and hell. Unless the youngsters in his charge were converted they would be eternally lost. Ann began to find the assumptions upon which she had based her life challenged. By the spring of 1806 a number of the eighty or so lively young people at the Academy had professed conversion. Their intensity of inner experience was profound. Many recorded these experiences in private journals; some exchanged lengthy and serious letters with other young people who had been similarly changed. Parents too were converted. A revival was taking place.

Events that summer in the peaceful New England town were just a cameo of what was taking place through towns and villages up and down America. Later, the great number of conversions and the huge increase in people formally joining the church would become known as the 'Second Great Awakening'. The colonies had witnessed the first 'Great Awakening' during the mid-eighteenth century, but it is estimated that in 1800 only 6.9% of the population were formally linked with a church.[1] At that time the population of the thirteen states was probably not much more than five million. Independence

North America: principal places associated with Ann Judson

had been recognized by Britain in 1783, and the treaty boundary was
the Mississippi River, the seeming limit of westward expansion. But
the nineteenth century would pose an unprecedented challenge to the
Christian church. As the frontier shifted westwards right over to the
Pacific Ocean, and as immigrants flooded in, the population shot up
to nearly ninety-two million by 1910. Would the nineteenth century
witness the evangelization of this rapidly increasing population? Or
would it be won over to modern notions of rationalism and humanism?

The answer is clear. By 1910, 43.5% of the population were formal
members of a church.[2] The nineteenth century was one of tremendous
expansion—for the Christian church, as well as for the nation. Much
of this expansion took place during significant revivals of religion at
the beginning and end of the century, the Second and Third Great
Awakenings. The Second Great Awakening lasted for at least the
first quarter of the nineteenth century. Revivals of religion occurred
in many states and in all Protestant denominations. In towns such as
Bradford the movement was undramatic, without hysteria, conversions
occurring in a 'calm and ordinary manner'.[3]

And thus, what happened to sixteen-year-old Ann Hasseltine in
1806 may be seen as part of a much larger movement. During the
same revival in Bradford her parents, brother and sisters were all
converted and formally joined the Congregational Church. One of
Ann's young friends, twelve-year old Harriet Atwood from nearby
Haverhill, was also converted. Ann and Harriet were not unusual in
their experience, but because they were soon to become two of the
first American missionaries, extracts from their diaries and letters
were kept and later published.[4] Ann described in her diary the effect
the revival had on her:

Harriet Newell
Harriet (then Harriet Atwood) was converted during the same
revival as Ann Judson. The two friends were later to sail together
as two of the first American women missionaries to foreign lands.

During the first sixteen years of my life, I very seldom felt any serious impressions, which I think were produced by the Holy Spirit. I was early taught by my mother (though she was then ignorant of the nature of true religion) the importance of abstaining from those vices to which children are liable—as telling falsehoods, disobeying my parents, taking what was not my own, etc. She also taught me, that if I were a good child, I should, at death, escape that dreadful hell, the thought of which sometimes filled me with alarm and terror. I therefore, made it a matter of conscience to avoid the above-mentioned sins, to say my prayers night and morning, and to abstain from my usual play on the Sabbath, not doubting but that such a course of conduct would ensure my salvation.

At the age of twelve or thirteen, I attended the academy at Bradford, where I was exposed to many more temptations than before, and found it much more difficult to pursue my pharisaical method. I now began to attend balls and parties of pleasure, and found my mind completely occupied with what I daily heard were 'innocent amusements.' My conscience reproved me, not for engaging in these amusements, but for neglecting to say my prayers and read my Bible, on returning from them; but I finally put a stop to its remonstrances, by thinking, that, as I was old enough to attend balls, I was surely too old to say prayers. Thus were my fears quieted; and for two or three years I scarcely felt an anxious thought relative to the salvation of my soul, though I was rapidly verging towards eternal ruin ... I was surrounded with associates, wild and volatile like myself, and often thought myself one of the happiest creatures on earth.

The first circumstance, which, in any measure, awakened me from this sleep of death, was the following. One Sabbath morning, having prepared myself to attend public worship ... I accidentally took up Hannah More's *Strictures on Female Education;*[5] and the first words that caught my eye were, *She that liveth in pleasure, is dead while she liveth.* They were written in italics, with marks of admiration; and they struck me to the heart. I stood for a few moments, amazed at the incident, and half inclined to think, that some invisible agency had directed my eye to these words. At first, I thought I would lead a different life, and be more serious and sedate; but at last I thought, that the words were not so applicable to me as I at first imagined, and resolved to think no more of them.

In the course of a few months (at the age of fifteen,) I met with Bunyan's *Pilgrim's Progress.* I read it as a Sabbath book, and was much interested in the story. I finished the book on a Sabbath, and it left this impression on my mind—that Christian, because he adhered to the narrow path, was carried safely through all his trials, and at last admitted into heaven. I resolved, from that moment, to begin a religious life; and in order to keep my resolution, I went to my chamber to pray for divine assistance. When I had done, I felt pleased with myself, and thought I was in a fair way for heaven. But I was perplexed to know what it was to live a religious life, and again had recourse to my system of works ...(17–19).

Thus began a struggle which lasted for months. Ann would resolve to give up parties; the resolution would be broken. She would sometimes weep with a realization of her sins, but would then throw herself back into her active social life:

From December 1805 to April 1806… My studies were slightly attended to, and my time was mostly occupied in preparing my dress, and in contriving amusements for the evenings, which portion of my time was wholly spent in vanity and trifling. I so far surpassed my friends in gaiety and mirth, that some of them were apprehensive that I had but a short time to continue in my career of folly, and should be suddenly cut off …

In the spring of 1806, there appeared a little attention to religion, in the upper parish of Bradford. Religious conferences had been appointed, during the winter, and I now began to attend them regularly. I often used to weep, when hearing the minister, and others, press the importance of improving the present favourable season, to obtain an interest in Christ, lest we should have to say, *The harvest is passed, the summer is ended, and we are not saved.* I thought I should be one of that number; for though I now deeply felt the importance of being strictly religious, it appeared to me impossible I could be so … (20).

In this bewildered frame of mind, Ann visited an aunt whom she knew to be a pious woman. She had not intended to discuss her own feelings, but in response to the woman's kindly enquiries burst into tears. She continued the account:

I then, for the first time in my life, communicated feelings which I had determined should be known to none but myself. She urged the importance of my cherishing those feelings, and of devoting myself entirely to seeking an interest in Christ, before it should be for ever too late. She told me, that if I trifled with impressions which were evidently made by the Holy Spirit, I should be left to hardness of heart and blindness of mind.

Her words penetrated my heart, and I felt resolved to give up every thing, and seek to be reconciled to God. That fear, which I had ever felt, that others would know that I was serious, now vanished away, and I was willing that the whole universe should know that I felt myself to be a lost and perishing sinner … I felt, that if I died in that situation, I must perish; but how to extricate myself I knew not. I had not been in the habit of reading religious books; I could not understand the Bible; and felt myself as perfectly ignorant of the nature of true religion, as the very heathen. In this extremity, the next morning, I ventured to ask the preceptor [her teacher] what I should do. He told me to pray for mercy, and submit myself to God. He also put into my hands some religious magazines, in which I read the conviction and conversion of some, who, I perceived, had once felt as I now felt. I shut myself up in my chamber, denied myself every innocent gratification, such as eating fruit and other things, not absolutely necessary to support life, and spent my days in reading and crying for mercy. But I had seen, as yet, very little of the awful wickedness of my heart. I knew not yet the force of that passage, *The carnal mind is enmity against God*. I thought myself very penitent, and almost prepared by voluntary abstinence, to receive the divine favour. After spending two or three weeks in this manner, without obtaining the least comfort, my heart began to rise in rebellion against God. I thought it unjust in him not to notice my prayers and my repentance. I could not endure the thought, that he was a sovereign God, and had a right to call one and leave another to perish. So far from being merciful in calling some, I thought it cruel in him to send any of his creatures to hell for their disobedience. But my chief distress was occasioned by a view of his perfect purity and holiness. My heart was filled with aversion and hatred towards a *holy* God; and I felt, that

if admitted into heaven, with the feelings I then had, I should
be as miserable as I could be in hell. In this state, I longed for
annihilation; and if I could have destroyed the existence of my
soul, with as much ease as that of my body, I should quickly have
done it. But that glorious Being, who is kinder to his creatures
than they are to themselves, did not leave me to remain long in
this distressing state. I began to discover a beauty in the way of
salvation by Christ. He appeared to be just such a Saviour as I
needed. I saw how God could be just, saving sinners through
him. I committed my soul into his hands, and besought him to
do with me what seemed good in his sight. When I was thus
enabled to commit myself into the hands of Christ, my mind was
relieved from that distressing weight which had borne it down
for so long a time. I did not think that I had obtained the new
heart, which I had been seeking, but felt happy in contemplating
the character of Christ, and particularly, that disposition which
led him to suffer so much, for the sake of doing the will and
promoting the glory of his heavenly Father. A few days after this,
as I was reading Bellamy's *True Religion,* I obtained a new view
of the character of God. His justice, displayed in condemning
the finally impenitent, which I had before viewed as cruel, now
appeared to be an expression of hatred to sin, and regard to the
good of beings in general. A view of his purity and holiness
filled my soul with wonder and admiration. I felt a disposition to
commit myself unreservedly into his hands, and leave it with him
to save me or cast me off, for I felt I could not be unhappy, while
allowed the privilege of contemplating and loving so glorious
a Being. I now began to hope, that I had passed from death
unto life. When I examined myself, I was constrained to own,
that I had feelings and dispositions to which I was formerly an
utter stranger. I had sweet communion with the blessed God,

from day to day; my heart was drawn out in love to Christians
of whatever denomination; the sacred Scriptures were sweet to
my taste; and such was my thirst for religious knowledge, that
I frequently spent a great part of the night in reading religious
books. O how different were my views of myself and of God,
from what they were, when I first began to enquire what I should
do to be saved! I felt myself to be a poor lost sinner, destitute of
every thing to recommend myself to the divine favour; that I was,
by nature, inclined to every evil way; and that it had been the
mere sovereign, restraining mercy of God, not my own goodness,
which had kept me from committing the most flagrant crimes.
This view of myself humbled me in the dust, melted me into
sorrow and contrition for my sins, induced me to lay my soul
at the feet of Christ, and plead his merits alone, as the ground
of my acceptance. I felt that if Christ had not died, to make an
atonement for sin, I could not ask God to dishonour his holy
government so far as to save so polluted a creature, and that
should he even now condemn me to suffer eternal punishment,
it would be so just, that my mouth would be stopped, and all
holy beings in the universe would acquiesce in the sentence, and
praise him, as a just and righteous God (21–4).

Such was Ann's conversion. She continued to be 'one of the happiest
creatures on earth', optimistic and cheerful in disposition, but now she
found happiness in something rather different from the socializing
which had previously been her delight. It is interesting to compare
her writing with that of Harriet Atwood. Harriet was also converted
in the religious revival of 1806 in Bradford and her journal is very
similar to Ann's. Harriet's correspondence shows that the intensity and
seriousness of Ann's experience were not unusual. What distinguished
Ann's writing, even at such an early age, as compared with Harriet's,

was her very articulate expression of her convictions regarding the sovereignty of God. She demonstrated a capacity to express profound theological truth in a clear and coherent manner—an ability which would prove invaluable later on.

2

'To improve the talents bestowed by God' (1806–1809)

Having experienced conversion, Ann was not content to remain passive; she was eager to serve others. She studied as hard as she could to prepare herself to become a teacher. We see something of the character of her commitment in the following extract from her journal, written while she was still sixteen:

My chief happiness now consisted in contemplating the moral perfections of the glorious God. I longed to have all intelligent creatures love him; and felt, that even fallen spirits could never be released from their obligations to love a Being possessed of such glorious perfections. I felt happy in the consideration, that so benevolent a Being governed the world, and ordered every passing event. I lost all disposition to murmur at any providence, assured that such a Being could not err in any dispensation. Sin, in myself and others, appeared as that abominable thing, which

a holy God hates,—and I earnestly strove to avoid sinning, not merely because I was afraid of hell, but because I feared to displease God, and grieve his Holy Spirit. I attended my studies in school, with far different feelings and different motives from what I had ever done before. I felt my obligation to improve all I had to the glory of God; and since he in his providence had favoured me with advantages for improving my mind, I felt that I should be like the slothful servant, if I neglected them. I, therefore, diligently employed all hours in school, in acquiring useful knowledge, and spent my evenings and part of the night in spiritual enjoyments.

While thus recounting the mercies of God to my soul, I am particularly affected by two considerations: the richness of that grace, which called and stopped me in my dangerous course, and the ungrateful returns I make for so distinguished a blessing. I am prone to forget the voice which called me out of darkness into light, and the hand which drew me from the horrible pit and the miry clay. When I first discerned my deliverer, my grateful heart offered him the services of a whole life, and resolved to acknowledge no other master. But such is the force of my native depravity, that I find myself prone to forsake him, grieve away his influence from my heart, and walk in the dark and dreary path of the backslider. I despair of making great attainments in the divine life, and look forward to death only, to free me from my sins and corruptions. Till that blessed period, that hour of my emancipation, I am resolved, through the grace and strength of my Redeemer, to maintain a constant warfare with my inbred sins, and endeavour to perform the duties incumbent on me, in whatever situation I may be placed (24–25).

Such a change was very obvious to all around. One friend wrote as follows:

> Redeeming love … was now her theme. One might spend days with her, without hearing any other subject reverted to. The throne of grace, too, was her early and late resort. I have known her to spend cold winter evenings in a chamber without fire, and return to the family with a solemnity spread over her countenance, which told of Him with whom she had been communing. Nor was her love of social pleasures diminished, although the complexion of them was completely changed (26).

The kind of socializing Ann now engaged in was this: 'after a season of prayer, proceeding to visit this and that family, to speak of him whom her soul loved'(26). She studied the Bible daily, using the works of Guise, Orton and Scott, and read Hopkins, Bellamy, Edwards, Doddridge and others, taking detailed notes of Jonathan Edwards' work on *Redemption*:

> With Edwards on Redemption, she was instructed, quickened, strengthened. Well do I remember the elevated smile which beamed on her countenance, when she first spoke to me of its precious contents. She had transcribed, with her own hand, Edwards' leading and most striking remarks on this great subject. When reading Scripture, sermons, or other works, if she met with any sentiment or doctrine, which seemed dark and intricate, she would mark it, and beg the first clergyman, who called at her father's, to elucidate and explain it (26–27).

Ann became a member of the Congregational Church in Bradford, and first took communion on 14 September 1806. It was common at

that time to draw up a list of resolutions, and Ann was no exception.
In contrast to the resolutions with which she had attempted to attain
salvation, these were formed in conscious dependence on the enabling
of God. On 3 November 1806 she recorded the following:

Spent the evening with my young religious friends and Mr.
P. whose conversation was remarkably solemn. He advised us
to make resolutions, for the government of our daily conduct.
I feel myself unable to keep any resolutions I may make; but
humbly relying on the grace of God for assistance, I will try. I
do desire to live wholly devoted to God, and to have every sin
in my heart entirely slain.

O thou God of all grace, I humbly beseech thee to enable me
to keep the following resolutions: When I first awake, solemnly
devote myself to God, for the day. Read several passages of
Scripture, and then spend as long time in prayer, as circumstances
permit. Read two chapters in the Old Testament, and one in the
New, and meditate thereon. Attend to the duties of my chamber.
If I have no needle-work to do, read in some religious book. At
school, diligently attend to the duties before me, and let not one
moment pass unimproved. At noon, read a portion of Scripture,
pray for the blessing of God, and spend the remainder of the
intermission, in reading some improving or religious book. In
all my studies, be careful to maintain an humble dependence on
divine assistance. In the evening, if I attend a religious meeting,
or any other place for instruction, before going, read a portion of
Scripture. If not, spend the evening in reading, and close the day as
I began. Resolve also to strive against the *first risings* of discontent,
fretfulness and anger; to be meek, and humble, and patient;
constantly to bear in mind, that I am in the presence of God;

habitually to look up to him for deliverance from temptations; and in all cases, to do to others as I would have them do to me (29–30).

Her journal records ups and downs, times of discouragement and self-doubt. A comparison of her journal with that of Harriet reveals similar sections lamenting backsliding. In 1807, Ann, now aged seventeen, wrote to a friend:

A person who grows in grace, will see more and more of the dreadful wickedness of his heart. He will find it more opposed to every thing good, more deceitful and fickle ... The more grace Christians have, the clearer they can see the contrast between holiness and sin; and while it leads them to hunger, thirst and strive for the one, it leads them to loath, abhor, and mourn for the other ... (34–35).

She described the beginning of her teaching career as follows:

Have taken charge of a few scholars. Ever since I have had a comfortable hope in Christ, I have desired to devote myself to him, in such a way, as to be useful to my fellow creatures. As Providence has placed me in a situation of life, where I have had an opportunity of getting as good an education as I desire, I feel it would be highly criminal in me not to improve it. I feel also, that it would be equally criminal to desire to be well educated and accomplished, from selfish motives, with a view merely to gratify my taste and relish for improvement, or my pride in being qualified to shine. I therefore resolved last winter, to attend the academy, from no other motive, than to improve the talents bestowed by God, so as to be more extensively devoted

to his glory, and the benefit of my fellow creatures. On being lately requested to take a small school, for a few months, I felt very unqualified to have the charge of little immortal souls; but the hope of doing them good, by endeavouring to impress their young and tender minds with divine truth, and the obligation I feel *to try to be useful*, have induced me to comply. I was enabled to open the school with prayer. Though the cross was very great, I felt constrained, by a sense of duty, to take it up. The little creatures seemed astonished at such a beginning. Probably some of them had never heard a prayer before. O may I have grace to be faithful, in instructing these little immortals, in such a way as shall be pleasing to my heavenly Father (36–7).

Similarly Harriet Atwood, aged eighteen, wrote in 1811 when starting a teaching position: 'Can I think of such a responsible situation as that of instructing little immortals? I know that I ought not to consult my own ease; the question should be, how can I be most useful in the world?'[1]

For several years Ann taught schools in Salem, Haverhill and Newbury. She took this work very seriously, regarding herself as entrusted with a responsibility for the souls of her students, and she prayed regularly for them.

Nor was she content to pray only for the conversion of those immediately in her care; her journal records a private and yet overwhelming desire that God should be glorified in conversions overseas. It is clear that she was being prepared for a missionary vocation:

March 17 [probably 1809]. Have had some enjoyment in reading the life of David Brainerd [pioneer missonary to the North American Indians]. It had a tendency to humble me, and excite desires to live as near to God, as that holy man did. Have spent this evening in prayer for quickening grace. Felt my heart enlarged to pray for spiritual blessings for myself, my friends, the church at large, the heathen world, and the African slaves. Felt a willingness to give myself away to Christ, to be disposed of as he pleases. Here I find safety and comfort. Jesus is my only refuge …

March 24. At the commencement of the last week, I had high hopes of being more engaged in religion, than ever before. But I have reason to fear, that I relied too much on my own strength. I still find cause to be humbled in the dust, for my inconstancy and rebellion. I have done little for the cause of God—too often indulged in trifling conversation. In this way I grieve the Holy Spirit, and bring darkness upon my mind. And yet I hope, that I have had some right feelings. I would not deny what I have enjoyed, though it is but small. I have, at times, felt engaged in prayer for the prosperity of the Church, and for the conversion of the heathen and Jews (39–40).

3

'How could we most promote the glory of God?' (1810–1812)

The Hasseltine household was often full of visitors. 28 June 1810 must have seemed much like any other day: lunch was to be provided for a group of Congregational ministers. Ann was now twenty-one; she and her sisters were often called upon to help entertain, which they no doubt did with grace and liveliness. On this day four students had appeared before the General Association of Congregational ministers in Bradford. These four were offering themselves for a lifetime of overseas missionary service, the first Americans ever to do so. One of the students was Adoniram Judson,[1] and he was among those who adjourned to Deacon Hasseltine's house in the middle of the day. Having gone through the trauma of presenting their case to the Association, Adoniram now faced another drama, his meeting with Ann. It seems that he was captivated immediately. Her sparkling personality and beauty were most immediately apparent, but it cannot have taken him long to discover her deep piety and her

Adoniram Judson

burning missionary concern. Just a month later he formally wrote to her, asking if they could commence a courtship. She replied that her father's permission would be needed. And thus Adoniram wrote perhaps the most extraordinary letter to a prospective father-in-law that has ever been composed:

> I have now to ask, whether you can consent to part with your daughter early next spring, to see her no more in this world; whether you can consent to her departure for a heathen land, and her subjection to the hardships and sufferings of a missionary life; whether you can consent to her exposure to the dangers of the ocean; to the fatal influence of the southern climate of India; to every kind of want and distress; to degradation, insult, persecution, and perhaps a violent death. Can you consent to all this, for the sake of him who left his heavenly home, and died for her and for you; for the sake of perishing, immortal souls; for the sake of Zion, and the glory of God? Can you consent to all this, in hope of soon meeting your daughter in the world of glory, with a crown of righteousness, brightened by the acclamations of praise which shall redound to her Saviour from the heathens saved, through her means, from eternal woe and despair? (52).

Amazingly, John and Rebecca Hasseltine left their youngest daughter to decide for herself. It will perhaps never be known how far Ann was swayed by love for Adoniram, and how far by her own highly developed burden for mission. Both no doubt played their part. What is certain is that there was very little encouragement from other quarters. Knowles wrote:

> No female had ever left America as a Missionary to the heathen. The general opinion was decidedly opposed to the measure. It

was deemed wild and romantic in the extreme; and altogether inconsistent with prudence and delicacy. Miss H. had no example to guide and allure her. She met with no encouragement from the greater part of those persons, to whom she applied for counsel. Some expressed strong disapprobation of the project. Others would give no opinion. Two or three ... were steady, affectionate advisers, and encouraged her to go. With these exceptions, she was forced to decide from her own convictions of duty, and her own sense of fitness and expediency.

It is well for the cause of missions, that God assigned to Miss Hasseltine the honourable yet difficult office of leading the way in this great enterprise. Her adventurous spirit, and her decision of character, eminently fitted her to resolve, where others would hesitate, and to advance where others might retreat. She did decide to go, and her determination, without doubt, has had some effect on the minds of other females, who have since followed her example [i.e. Harriet Atwood, who married Samuel Newell, and Roxana Peck, who married Samuel Nott] (46).

The very novelty of the idea of going to Asia as missionaries probably meant that the 'general opinion' was viciously opposed. By the spring of 1811 the amazement may have died down somewhat, so that when young Harriet Atwood made a similar decision she could write in May 1811:

> *All* my friends with whom I have conversed since my return to Haverhill, advise me to go. Some Christians who were formerly opposed, after obtaining a more extensive knowledge of the subject, think females would be useful.[2]

Ann's journal at this time reveals the extreme difficulty of the decision before her:

> *Aug. 8, 1810.* Endeavoured to commit myself entirely to God, to be disposed of, according to his pleasure. He is now trying my faith and confidence in him, by presenting dark and gloomy prospects, that I may be enabled, through divine grace, to gain an ascendancy over my selfish and rebellious spirit, and prefer the will of God to my own. I do feel, that his service is my delight. Might I but be the means of converting a single soul, it would be worth spending all my days to accomplish. Yes, I feel willing to be placed in that situation, in which I can do most good, *though it were to carry the Gospel to the distant, benighted heathen.*

> *Sept. 10.* For several weeks past, my mind has been greatly agitated. An opportunity has been presented to me, of spending my days among the heathen, in attempting to persuade them to receive the Gospel. Were I convinced of its being a call from God, and that it would be more pleasing to him, for me to spend my life in this way than in any other, I think I should be willing to relinquish every earthly object, and in full view of dangers and hardships, give myself up to the great work.

> A consideration of this subject has occasioned much self-examination, to know on what my hopes were founded, and whether my love to Jesus was sufficiently strong to induce me to forsake all for his cause. At times I have felt satisfied, that I loved him on account of his own glorious perfections, and have been desirous that he should do with me as he should please, and place me in that situation, in which I can be most useful. I have felt great satisfaction in committing this case to God, knowing,

that he has a perfect understanding of the issue of all events, is infinitely wise to select the means best calculated to bring about the most important ends, and is able and willing to make the path of duty plain before me, and incline me to walk therein. At other times, I have felt ready to sink, being distressed with fears about my spiritual state, and appalled at the prospect of pain and suffering, to which my nature is so averse, and apprehensive, that when assailed by temptation, or exposed to danger and death, I should not be able to endure, as seeing Him who is invisible. But I now feel willing to leave it entirely with God ...

Oct. 28. My mind has still been agitated for two or three weeks past, in regard to the above-mentioned subject. But I have, at all times, felt a disposition to leave it with God, and trust in him to direct me. I have at length come to the conclusion, that if nothing in providence appears to prevent, I must spend my days in a heathen land. I am a creature of God, and he has an undoubted right to do with me, as seemeth good in his sight. I rejoice, that I am in his hands—that he is every where present, and can protect me in one place as well as in another. He has my heart in his hands, and when I am called to face danger, to pass through scenes of terror and distress, he can inspire me with fortitude, and enable me to trust in him. Jesus is faithful; his promises are precious. Were it not for these considerations, I should with my present prospects sink down in despair, especially as no female has, to my knowledge, ever left the shores of America, to spend her life among the heathen; nor do I yet know, that I shall have a single female companion. But God is my witness, that I have not dared to decline the offer that has been made me, though so many are ready to call it a 'wild romantic undertaking.' If I have been deceived in thinking it my duty to go to the heathen,

I humbly pray, that I may be undeceived, and prevented from going. But whether I spend my days in India or America, I desire to spend them in the service of God, and be prepared to spend an eternity in his presence. O Jesus, make me live to thee, and I desire no more (47–9).

Three days before the meeting with Samuel Newell which would similarly change Harriet's whole life, Harriet wrote in her diary of a visit from Ann:

> *October 20th 1810:* A female friend called upon us this morning. She informed me of her determination to quit her native land, to endure the sufferings of a Christian among heathen nations—to spend her days in India's sultry clime. How did this news affect my heart! Is she willing to do all this for God; and shall I refuse to lend my little aid in a land where divine revelation has shed its clearest rays? I have *felt* more, for the salvation of the Heathen, this day, than I recollect to have felt through my whole past life.[3]

Some further extracts from Ann's diary give a glimpse of her spiritual state at this time:

> *Nov. 25* [*1810*]. ... When I get near to God, and discern the excellence of the character of the Lord Jesus, and especially his power and willingness to save, I feel desirous, that the whole world should become acquainted with this Saviour. I am not only willing to spend my days among the heathen, in attempting to enlighten and save them, but I find much pleasure in the prospect. Yes, I am quite willing to give up temporal comforts, and live a life of hardship and trial, if it be the will of God.

Sabbath [*undated*]. ... This evening, attended a female prayer meeting. Felt solemn and engaged in prayer. Longed for clearer views of God, and stronger confidence in him. Made a new dedication of myself to God. Felt perfectly willing to give up my friends and earthly comforts, provided I might, in exile, enjoy the presence of God. I never felt more engaged in prayer for special grace, to prepare me for my great undertaking, than this evening. I am confident God will support me in every trying hour. I have strong hope, that in giving me such an opportunity of labouring for him, he will make me peculiarly useful. No matter where I am, if I do but serve the infinitely blessed God; and it is my comfort, that he can prepare me to serve him. Blessed Jesus, I am thine for ever. Do with me what thou wilt; lead me in the path in which thou wouldest have me to go, and it is enough.

Nov. 23. My heart has been quite revived, this evening, with spiritual things. Had some views of the excellent nature of the kingdom of Christ. Longed, above all things, to have it advanced. Felt an ardent desire to be instrumental of spreading the knowledge of the Redeemer's name, in a heathen land. Felt it a great, an undeserved privilege, to have an opportunity of going. Yes, I think I should rather go to India, among the heathen, notwithstanding the almost insurmountable difficulties in the way, than to stay at home and enjoy the comforts and luxuries of life. Faith in Christ will enable me to persevere in my purpose. O, if he will condescend to make me useful in promoting his kingdom, I care not where I perform his work, nor how hard it be. *Behold the handmaid of the Lord; be it unto me according to thy word* (50–51).

A letter to her friend Lydia Kimball, written on 8 September 1810, summarizes her sense of 'call':

I feel willing, and expect, if nothing in providence prevent, to spend my days in this world in heathen lands. Yes, Lydia, I have about come to the determination to give up all my comforts and enjoyments here, sacrifice my affection to relatives and friends, and go where God, in his providence, shall see fit to place me. My determinations are not hasty, or formed without viewing the dangers, trials, and hardships attendant on a missionary life. Nor were my determinations formed in consequence of an attachment to an earthly object; but with a sense of my obligations to God, and with a full conviction of its being a call in providence, and consequently my duty (54).

On New Year's Day, 1811, Adoniram wrote to Ann as follows:

It is with the utmost sincerity, and with my whole heart, that I wish you, my love, a happy new year. May it be a year in which your walk will be close with God; your frame calm and serene; and the road that leads you to the Lamb marked with purer light. May it be a year in which you will have more largely the spirit of Christ, be raised above sublunary things, and be willing to be disposed of in this world just as God shall please. As every moment of the year will bring you nearer the end of your pilgrimage, may it bring you nearer to God, and find you more prepared to hail the messenger of death as a deliverer and a friend. And now, since I have begun to wish, I will go on. May this be the year in which you will change your name; in which you will take a final leave of your relatives and native land; in which you will cross the wide ocean, and dwell on the other side

of the world, among a heathen people. What a great change will this year probably effect in our lives![4]

4

'The trying scene of parting' (1812)

Sea travellers at the beginning of the nineteenth century were dependent on the wind for power. Paddle steamers were used on rivers such as the Mississippi, but the huge coal consumption of such vessels meant they would not be used for ocean routes until the 1830s. The journey by sea from America to England could take just over a month; the journey to India would take about four months. Without refrigeration, live animals and poultry were kept on board for meat, and the problem of carrying sufficient fresh food and water for the long journey was immense. Conditions on board were unpleasant, and the ocean itself was hazardous. Back in 1806 Ann's only brother had been lost at sea. Moreover, sea travel at this time involved dangers from enemy ships. The war between France and Britain from 1793 to 1815 involved naval battles over disputed overseas territories. Between 1812 and 1814 Britain was also at war with America.

In this unpromising context, the whole of 1811 was spent in attempts to organize the fledgling mission. First, Adoniram left for England on

11 January. He was to explore the possibility of the London Missionary Society's helping the American Congregationalists with the new mission venture. The ship on which Adoniram travelled was captured by the French. He and all the passengers were taken prisoner on board *L'Invincible Napoleon* and he subsequently experienced an unpleasant period of detention in France. Eventually, however, he gained his freedom, and arrived in England in May 1811. There he offered himself and three colleagues (Newell, Nott and Hall, plus the three wives) to work with the London Missionary Society if funds were not forthcoming from America. Sailing from Gravesend on 18 June, he arrived back in New York on 7 August.

In September the Congregational Board met again. They vacillated. Some believed the whole venture should be postponed because of the imminent war between America and England. Adoniram decided to force the issue. He and Nott declared that if the board did not send them straight away, then they would go, supported by the London Missionary Society. This was sufficient. The board appointed Judson, Nott, Newell and Hall as missionaries to Asia. A fifth man, Luther Rice, would soon be added to the number. Some regarded Adoniram's determination as commendable; others saw his action as virtual blackmail.

Preparations had to be made swiftly. As war with England became more and more likely, America was placed under blockade. Once a ship was found going to India, it would have to be taken as it might be the last for a long time. Late in January 1812, news came that a ship was to sail for Calcutta in a fortnight. Ordination services were fixed for 6 February and whirlwind preparations were made, including a frantic collection of funds.

On 5 February 1812, Ann and Adoniram were married in the room in the Hasseltine house in which they had met. During these final days, Ann's young friend Harriet, aged only eighteen, married Samuel Newell. Also on 5 February there was an emotional farewell service for the two girls in Haverhill church. Parson Allan had known Ann and Harriet since they were toddlers. He gave a solemn charge and composed a hymn for the occasion. There were few dry eyes, for all knew that this was a final farewell. In all probability these girls would never see their families and friends again, and none knew what lay ahead of them.

There was a larger and even more emotionally charged service the next day. Ann had by now said her goodbyes to her family—her parents and three sisters, Rebecca, Mary and Abigail. The ordination of the missionaries was to take place in Salem. The Tabernacle there was packed, with maybe as many as 2,000 squeezed in. From the beginning of the service the gathering was hushed, 'as still as death', but when the ordination took place 'an irresistible sighing and weeping' broke out, and from this moment, 'The entire wrapt congregation seemed moved as the trees of the wood are moved by a mighty wind. Pent-up emotion could no longer be restrained.'[1] The historic significance of this service cannot be overestimated: America was sending abroad the first of what was to become, to date, the mightiest missionary force in Christian history.

The ordination service having taken place on 6 February, it was found that places on two vessels were available. Due to the hazards of the ocean it would be prudent for the missionaries to travel in two groups. On 18 February, Samuel and Roxana Nott, Gordon Hall and Luther Rice sailed in the *Harmony* from Philadelphia. The *Harmony* arrived in Calcutta on 8 August—a trip of nearly six months. Ann

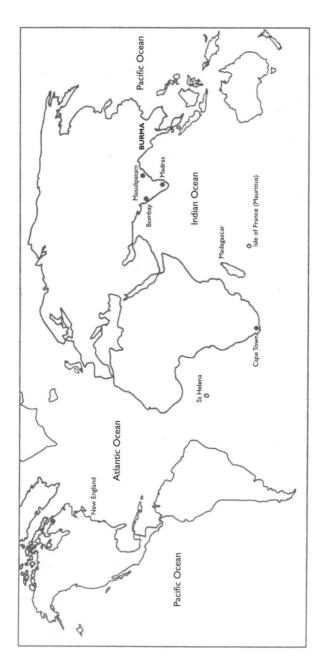

The World of the Nineteenth Century

and Adoniram Judson and Samuel and Harriet Newell moved on board the *Caravan* on 18 February, but had to wait for favourable winds before they set sail from Salem the next day. The *Caravan*, a two-masted ship with square-rigged sails, made better time than the *Harmony*; it took four months to cross the Atlantic, round the Cape of Good Hope, and sail up to Calcutta, finally arriving on 18 June 1812. Ann recorded the departure as follows:

Feb. 18. Took leave of my friends and native land, and embarked on board the brig *Caravan,* for India. Had so long anticipated the trying scene of parting, that I found it more tolerable than I feared. Still my heart bleeds. O America, my native land, must I leave thee? Must I leave my parents, my sisters and brothers, my friends beloved, and all the scenes of my early youth? ... Yes, I must leave you all, for a heathen land, an uncongenial clime. Farewell, happy, happy scenes,—but never, no, never to be forgotten.

Feb. 19. Sea-sick all day, and unable to do anything. My thoughts, more than usual, fixed on divine things. Longed for the enjoyment of God's presence on our passage, that we may be preparing for usefulness in future life. In the night, had many distressing apprehensions of death. Felt unwilling to die on the sea, not so much on account of my state after death, as the dreadfulness of perishing amid the waves.

Feb. 21. Somewhat relieved from sickness, and able to read a few chapters in the Bible. Never had a greater sense of our obligations to live devoted to God, resulting from his distinguished mercies. Even on the ocean, confined as I am, I find many sources of

enjoyment, and feel as happy as when on land, in the midst of my friends.

Feb. 22. O for a heart to live near to God, and serve him faithfully. I need nothing so much as ardent piety. I should feel happy in the consideration of having left my native land, and my father's house, if, by making this sacrifice, the kingdom of Christ would be promoted. May it be my great object to live a useful, holy life, and prepare to die a peaceful death.

Feb. 27. This day has been regarded by our friends on land as a day of fasting and prayer for the prosperity of this mission, and I hope the same object has not been forgotten by us on the sea. I spent some time this evening on deck. The weather was pleasant; the motion of the vessel gentle, though rapid; the full moon shone clearly on the water; and all things around conspired to excite pleasing though melancholy sensations. My native land, my home, my friends, and all my forsaken enjoyments, rushed into my mind; my tears flowed profusely, and I could not be comforted. Soon, however, the consideration of having left all these for the dear cause of Christ, and the hope of being, one day, instrumental of leading some poor degraded females, to embrace him as their Saviour, soothed my griefs, dried up my tears, and restored peace and tranquillity to my mind.

March 14. ... I desire no higher enjoyment in this life than to be instrumental of leading some poor, ignorant heathen females to the knowledge of the Saviour. To have a female praying society, consisting of those who were once in heathen darkness, is what my heart earnestly pants after, and makes a constant subject of

prayer. Resolved to keep this in view, as one principal object of my life (57–61).

A letter to her sister hints at her happiness with Adoniram:

April 11, 1812. I find Mr. Judson one of the kindest, most faithful, and affectionate of husbands. His conversation frequently dissipates the gloomy clouds of spiritual darkness which hang over my mind, and brightens my hope of a happy eternity. I hope God will make us instrumental of preparing each other for usefulness in this world, and greater happiness in a future world (62).

A letter to her friend Lydia written in May gives further glimpses of life on board and the need to attend to physical as well as spiritual health:

The change of the weather in so short a time was so great, together with sea-sickness and the want of exercise, that I soon lost all relish for my food. Every thing tasted differently from what it does on land, and those things I was the most fond of at home, I loathed the most here. But I soon began to find the real cause of my ill health. It was want of exercise. For some time we could invent nothing which could give us exercise equal to what we had been accustomed to. Jumping the rope was finally invented, and this we found to be of great use. I began, and jumped it several times in the day, and found my health gradually return, until I was perfectly well. I mention these particulars, that *you*, should you ever go to sea, may escape ill health. I never enjoyed more perfect health in my life, than I do now; and I attribute it to my exercising so much.

We found it exceedingly hot the first time that we crossed the equator. When going round the Cape of Good Hope, we had rough, rainy weather for twenty days. I never knew till then 'the dangers of the deep.' I never felt before, my entire dependence on God for preservation. Some nights I never slept on account of the rocking of the vessel and the roaring of the winds. Yet God preserved us—enabled us to trust in him and feel safe. Surely we have every reason to confide in God, and leave it with him to dispose of us as he pleases ... I have spent the most of my time, since on the water, in reading. I knew I needed a more intimate acquaintance with the sacred Scriptures; consequently, I have confined my attention almost exclusively to them. I have read the New Testament once through in course, two volumes of Scott's Commentary on the Old, Paley, Trumbull, and Dick, on the Inspiration of the Scriptures, together with Faber and Smith on the Prophecies. I have been much interested in reading these authors on inspiration, on account of my almost total ignorance of the evidence of the divinity of the Scriptures, and I gained fresh evidences of the reality of the Christian religion (63–5).

Despite Ann's cheerful tone, this was not the most pleasant of honeymoons, and overshadowing all was the sense of entering the unknown; there was no certain field of labour mapped out for them, no guarantee that they would be allowed to begin the work of spreading the gospel as they longed to do. But through Ann's letters and journals there is the quiet certainty that God is sovereign. She believed that although they did not know what lay ahead, he most certainly did. Such implicit faith in God's control over all things—from the waves on the sea to the hearts of governors—was what enabled them to enjoy even such a cramped and uncomfortable voyage into the unknown.

5

'Perplexed, but not in despair'
(1812–1813)

To the delight of all, land was sighted on 14 June. First impressions of India were faithfully recorded in a letter to Ann's sister:

> Day before yesterday, we came in sight of land, after being out only one hundred and twelve days. We could distinguish nothing on land except the towering mountains of Golconda. Yesterday morning, we were nearer land, and could easily discover the trees on the shore. Some appeared to be placed regularly in rows, others were irregular and scattered. The scene was truly delightful, and reminded me of the descriptions I have read, of the fertile shores of India—the groves of orange and palm trees. I likewise thought it probable, that these shores were inhabited by a race of beings, by nature like ourselves, but who, not like us, are ignorant of the God who made them, and the Saviour who died for them …

Tuesday. ... the scene is now truly delightful. We are sailing up the river Hoogly, a branch of the Ganges, and so near the land, that we can distinctly discover objects. On one side of us are the sunderbunds—[islands at the mouths of the Ganges]. The smell which proceeds from them, is fragrant beyond description. We have passed the mango trees, and some large brick houses.

Wednesday. I have never, my dear sister, witnessed or read any thing so delightful as the present scene. On each side of the Hoogly, where we are now sailing, are the Hindoo cottages, as thick together as the houses in our sea-ports. They are very small, and in the form of hay-stacks, without either chimneys or windows. They are situated in the midst of trees, which hang over them, and appear truly romantic. The grass and fields of rice are perfectly green, and herds of cattle are every where feeding on the banks of the river. The pagodas we have passed are much handsomer and larger than the houses. Notwithstanding the scene is so pleasant, on account of the works of nature, yet it is truly melancholy when we reflect, that these creatures, so numerous, so harmless, have immortal souls, and like us are destined to the eternal world—and yet have none to tell them of Christ ...

Well, Abigail, here we are safe in Calcutta harbour, and almost stunned with the noise of the natives. Mr. Judson has got on shore, to find a place for us to go. This city is by far the most elegant of any thing I have ever seen. Many ships are lying at anchor, and hundreds of natives all around. They are dressed very curiously with white, hanging loosely over their shoulders. But I have not time to describe any thing at present. We have plenty of fruit on board. The bananas are a very delicious fruit; they taste much like a rich pear.

Thursday. Harriet and I are yet on board the vessel, and have
not been on land. Mr. Judson did not return last night, until the
evening, and had not gained permission from the Police office to
live in the country, consequently we could not go on shore. Mr. J.
and Mr. N. are gone again today, and what will be their success
I know not. The East India Company are violently opposed to
missions, and have barely given liberty to their own countrymen
to settle here as preachers. We have nothing to expect from man,
and every thing from God ... (66–9).

On 18 June Ann and Harriet were able to leave the ship, and were
invited to stay with the British Baptist missionary William Carey. They
spent one night in his Calcutta home before leaving for Serampore,
the main base for the British Baptist mission. The Judsons and Newells
were invited to stay at Serampore until the other American missionaries
arrived. (The *Harmony* arrived six weeks after the *Caravan*.)Ann wrote
to her sister:

Mr. Judson came on board with an invitation from Dr. Carey
to spend the night with him. I got into a palankeen [covered
litter]—Mr. Judson walked to the house. It was with considerable
fear I rode, as the streets were full of natives and English carriages.
Those who carried me went so much faster than Mr. Judson, that
I soon lost sight of him, and did not know where they would
carry me. They, however, stopped before a large stone building,
which I soon found to be Dr. Carey's house. We were directed
up a pair of stairs, through one or two large rooms, into his study.
He arose, shook hands with us, and gave us a cordial welcome
to this country. His house is curiously constructed, as the other
European houses are here. There are no chimneys or fire-places in
them, the roofs are flat, the rooms are twenty feet in height, and

proportionably large. Large windows, without glass, open from
one room to another, that the air may freely circulate through
the house. They are very convenient for this hot climate, and bear
every mark of antiquity. In the evening we attended meeting
in the English Episcopal Church. It was the first time of our
attending meeting for above four months, and as we entered
the church, our ears were delighted with hearing the organ play
our old favourite tune, Bangor. The church was very handsome,
and a number of punkies, something like a fan several yards in
length, hung around, with ropes fastened to the outside, which
were pulled by some of the natives, to keep the church cool. We
spent the night at Dr. Carey's, and were rejoiced to find ourselves
once more in a house on land. Very near the house, is a charity
school supported by this mission, in which are instructed two
hundred boys, and nearly as many girls …

In the afternoon, we left Calcutta, for Serampore, having
previously received an invitation from the Missionaries to reside
with them, until our brethren arrive. We were met at the water
side by Messrs. Marshman and Ward, who led us to the house,
and introduced us to their wives. They received us very cordially.
The school kept by Mrs. Marshman consists almost entirely of
the children belonging to the mission, and European young
ladies. They are taught various kinds of needle-work, embroidery,
etc., and study the languages. Mrs. Marshman's eldest daughter,
fourteen years of age, reads and writes Bengalee and English; and
has advanced some way in Latin, Greek, and Hebrew. The three
families live in separate houses, but all eat together, in a large
hall in the mission house … These Missionaries are eminently
pious as well as learned. The garden is as far superior to any in
America, as the best garden in America is to a common farmer's.

It consists of several acres, under the highest state of cultivation. Fruits of various kinds, plants, flowers, and vegetables, grow here in great abundance. The pine-apple grows on a low bush, the plantain on a tall stalk, and the cocoa-nut on a high tree, resembling our pine-tree.

The third day after we came here, there was a celebration of the worship of Juggernaut. We went about ten in the morning. The immense multitude of natives assembled on the occasion, and the noise they made, answered to the account Buchanan gave. The idol was set on the top of a stone building. He is only a lump of wood, his face painted with large black eyes, and a large red mouth. He was taken from his temple, and water poured on him to bathe him. This is introductory to a more solemn act of worship, which will be performed a fortnight hence. After these poor deluded creatures had bathed their god, they proceeded to bathe themselves. Poor, miserable, deluded beings, they know not what they do. O Mary! the inhabitants of America know nothing of poverty, slavery and wretchedness, compared with the natives of India. So very numerous, they cannot get employ; and when they do, they are treated by Europeans like beasts more than like men. Many of them die for the want of nourishment. Add to all this, they are ignorant of the only way of salvation. Who would not pity the poor heathen, and rejoice to contribute their mite to relieve some of their distress! (70–73).

Ann's pity would have been excited by descriptions of the rituals which regularly took place at the temple of Juggernaut (or Jagannath), 'Lord of the Universe', the local name of the Hindu god, Vishnu. During festivals, images were taken out of the temple on huge wooden carts (some fifty feet tall), sometimes drawn by 4,000 or so men.[1]

(Hence the modern usage of 'juggernaut' for a huge lorry.) In the 'swinging' ritual:

> ... two iron flesh hooks were pierced into the back of the devotee. Then, suspended by ropes attached to the hooks, he would be drawn some 40 feet in the air and twirled around for a considerable time. Sometimes the hooks gave way and the victim plummeted to his death. At Puri there was a car devoted for the god Jagannath which was pulled by means of hooks fastened into the flesh of the disciples. Numerous individuals were crushed to death beneath the wheels of the Jagannath car. Such frenzied acts were committed in hopes of making a self-atonement, thereby securing release from the cycle of existence.[2]

Despite the shock of their first exposure to Eastern religion, the Judsons were preoccupied at this time with two immediate dilemmas. The first was the question of where they should settle. About ten days after their arrival they received an order from the government to leave and return to America. Unfortunately, they had arrived in Calcutta just as war broke out between England and America. Moreover, the British East India Company[3] was adamantly opposed to Christian mission. The Christian message was potentially inflammatory and the company placed a premium on political and social stability.[4] Every door into neighbouring countries likewise seemed to be shut tight. Judson and Newell considered, but had to reject, the possibilities of Japan, Persia, Madagascar and even South America! The country which had first fascinated Adoniram, the country of Burma, was implacably opposed to Christian mission. The only possibility seemed to be Mauritius, or the Isle of France as it was then known, an island beyond the control of the British East India company, 5,000 miles away near Madagascar (see page 48). A ship was due to sail from Calcutta to Port Louis,

the capital of the Isle of France, on 1 August 1812. As only two places were available, the Newells took precedence so that they could get settled before the imminent arrival of Harriet's baby. Four days after the departure of the Newells, the *Harmony* arrived at Calcutta bringing Gordon Hall, Luther Rice and Samuel and Roxana Nott.

Ann and Adoniram spent the next couple of months in Calcutta. It was a time of suspense lest the East India Company enforce their deportation before they had been able to make their way to join the Newells.

They now had time to confront and resolve the second of their dilemmas. This was the change of conviction about baptism that led Adoniram and Ann to sever their links with their sending agency, the Congregational Church of America. Such a major shift in belief had begun with intensive studies during the voyage to India. Ann wrote to her friend Nancy:

An examination of the subject commenced on board the *Caravan*. As Mr. Judson was continuing the translation of the New Testament, which he began in America, he had many doubts concerning the word *baptize*. This, with the idea of meeting the Baptist brethren at Serampore, when he would wish to defend his own sentiments, induced a more thorough examination of the Pedobaptist system. The more he examined, the more his doubts increased; and unwilling as he was to admit it, he was *afraid* the Baptists were right and he wrong. After we arrived at Calcutta, his attention was turned from this subject to the concerns of the mission, and the difficulties with government. But as his mind was still uneasy, he again renewed the subject. I felt afraid he would become a Baptist, and frequently urged the unhappy consequences

if he should. But he said his duty compelled him to satisfy his own mind, and embrace those sentiments which appeared most concordant with Scripture. I always took the Pedobaptist side in reasoning with him, even after I was as doubtful of the truth of that system as he. We left Serampore to reside in Calcutta a week or two before the arrival of our brethren; and as we had nothing in particular to occupy our attention, we confined it exclusively to this subject. We procured the best authors on both sides, compared them with the Scriptures, examined and re-examined the sentiments of Baptists and Pedobaptists, and were finally compelled, from a conviction of truth, to embrace the former. Thus, my dear Nancy, we are confirmed Baptists, not because we wished to be, but because truth compelled us to be. We have endeavoured to count the cost, and be prepared for the many severe trials resulting from this change of sentiment. We anticipate the loss of reputation, and of the affection and esteem of many of our American friends. But the most trying circumstances attending this change, and that which has caused most pain, is the separation which must take place between us and our dear missionary associates. Although we are attached to each other, and should doubtless live very happily together, yet the brethren do not think it best we should unite in one mission. These things, my dear Nancy, have caused us to weep and pour out our hearts in prayer to Him whose directions we so much wish and need. We feel that we are alone in the world, with no real friend but each other, no one on whom we can depend but God.[5]

In fact Ann was far more reluctant to take this step than Adoniram. She probably felt far more intensely the personal embarrassment of repudiating the belief of her family and friends, and the cost, in terms

of relationships, of dividing from their missionary colleagues. She wrote to her parents:

> I tried to have him give it up, and rest satisfied in his old sentiments, and frequently told him, if he became a Baptist, *I would not*. He, however, said it was his duty to examine closely a subject on which he had so many doubts.[6]

An extract from her diary on 10 August 1812 describes the trauma this caused:

> *Aug. 10.* Besides the trials occasioned by the orders of government, I see another heavy trial just coming upon me. Mr. J's mind has been for some time much exercised in regard to baptism. He has been lately examining the subject more closely. All his prejudices are in favour of Pedobaptism; but he wishes to know the truth, and be guided in the path of duty. If he should renounce his former sentiments, he must offend his friends at home, hazard his reputation, and, what is still more trying, be separated from his missionary associates.

> [*Aug.*] *23.* I have been much distressed the week past, in the view of the probable separation between our missionary brethren and ourselves. Mr. J. feels convinced from Scripture, that he has never been baptized, and that he cannot conscientiously administer baptism to infants. This change of sentiment must necessarily produce a separation. As we are perfectly united with our brethren in every other respect, and are much attached to them, it is inexpressibly painful to leave them, and go alone to a separate station. But every sacrifice that duty requires, must be made. I do not myself feel satisfied on the subject of baptism,

having never given it a thorough examination. But I see many difficulties in the Pedobaptist theory, and must acknowledge that the face of Scripture does favour the Baptist sentiments. I intend to persevere in examining the subject, and hope that I shall be disposed to embrace the truth, whatever it may be. It is painfully mortifying to my natural feelings, to think seriously of renouncing a system which I have been taught from infancy to believe and respect, and embrace one which I have been taught to despise. O that the Spirit of God may enlighten and direct my mind—may prevent my retaining an old error, or embracing a new one!

Sept. 1. I have been examining the subject of baptism for some time past, and, contrary to my prejudices and my wishes, am compelled to believe, that believers' baptism alone is found in Scripture. If ever I sought to know the truth; if ever I looked up to the Father of lights; if ever I gave up myself to the inspired word, I have done so during this investigation. And the result is, that, laying aside my former prejudices and systems, and fairly appealing to the Scriptures, I feel convinced that nothing really can be said in favour of infant baptism or sprinkling. We expect soon to be baptized. O may our hearts be prepared for that holy ordinance! and as we are baptized into a profession of Christ, may we put on Christ, and walk worthy of the high vocation wherewith we are called. But in consequence of our performance of this duty, we must make some very painful sacrifices. We must be separated from our dear missionary associates, and labour alone in some isolated spot. We must expect to be treated with contempt, and cast off by many of our American friends—forfeit the character we have in our native land, and probably have to labour for our own support, wherever we are stationed (89–90).

Views of the Lal Bazaar Chapel, Calcutta,
where the Judsons were baptized

Ann and Adoniram were baptized by immersion in the Lal Bazaar Baptist Chapel in Calcutta on 6 September 1812. William Ward, colleague of William Carey, conducted the service.

Adoniram then had to write to the body that had sent him:

> The Board will, undoubtedly, feel as unwilling to support a Baptist missionary as I feel to comply with their instructions, which particularly direct us to baptize *'credible believers with their households'*... I have now the prospect before me of going alone to some distant island, unconnected with any society at present existing … Whether the Baptist churches in America will compassionate my situation, I know not ...'[7]

He then addressed another letter to Dr Bolles, a Salem Baptist minister:

> Under these circumstances, I look to you. Alone, in this foreign, heathen land, I make my appeal to those whom, with their permission, I will call *my Baptist brethren* in the United States (92).

These letters having been written, Ann and Adoniram had to resign themselves to the prospect of months, if not years, of delay before any response could be expected. They did not hear that they were to be supported by Baptists in America until September 1815—three years of uncertainty!

They were not to be quite alone. On 1 November, Luther Rice was similarly baptized. He too had fought against this decision, and Carey wrote:

Brother Rice was, on the voyage, thought by our brethren to be the most obstinate friend of Pedobaptism of any of the missionaries. I cannot tell what has led to this change of sentiment, nor had I any suspicion of it (93).

The first of the two dilemmas facing them, that concerning their future sphere of service, was soon to resurface in a dramatic way. In November 1812 they received a further ultimatum from the East India Company: they were to leave for London forthwith. It seemed that their missionary career was over before it had started.

6

'Harriet is dead' (1813)

The Judsons and Luther Rice had to make their escape from Calcutta. After various false starts they eventually got places on the *Creole*, which set sail for the Isle of France at the beginning of December 1812. The other missionaries had in the meantime sailed for Bombay.

The *Creole* was at sea for six weeks or so, during which time Ann and the others worked at learning French. When they arrived at the Isle of France on 17 January 1813 it was to devastating news, as Ann wrote in her diary:

> *Jan. 17, 1813.* Have at last arrived in port; but O what news, what distressing news! Harriet is dead. Harriet, my dear friend, my earliest associate in the Mission, is no more …
>
> [*Jan.*] *18.* Brother Newell has just been on board. Poor, disconsolate, broken-hearted widower. He has borne his afflictions

alone, without a single Christian friend to comfort his heart. His feelings allow him to give us a few broken hints only of Harriet's death. Poor girl, she suffered much. She became a mother on board ship, where she was exposed to the wet weather, and took a cold, which terminated in consumption. She died tranquil and happy, longing for the hour of her release. And she is happy now—all her trials over—all her tears wiped away. She is gone, and I am left behind, still to endure the trials of a missionary life. O that this severe dispensation may be sanctified to my soul; and may I be prepared to follow my dear departed sister.

[*Jan.*] *23.* No prospect of remaining long on this island. It seems as if there was no resting place for me on earth. O when will my wanderings terminate? When shall I find some little spot, that I can call my home, while in this world? Yet I rejoice in all thy dealings, O my heavenly Father; for thou dost support me under every trial, and enable me to lean on thee (95–6).

Harriet's baby had died at sea, and thus Samuel had lost a daughter as well as a wife. Ann had lost her friend and the Judsons were no nearer finding a place where they could work unhindered. They found that the grip of the slave owners in the Isle of France was such that no mission could conceivably be started there.

An extract from a letter to Ann's sisters illustrates the abject situation of the slaves in such a community:

Isle of France—Port Louis, March 12, 1813.

My dear Sisters,

A circumstance took place this evening, the recital of which, I think, will interest your feelings, and which greatly encourages *me* to plead the cause of humanity whenever an opportunity offers. Last night I heard a considerable noise in the yard in which we live, connected with another family. We went to the door, and saw a female slave with her hands tied behind her, and her mistress beating her with a club, in a most dreadful manner. My blood run cold within me, and I could quietly see it no longer. I went up to the mistress, and in broken French, asked her to stop, and what her servant had done. She immediately stopped, and told me that her servant was very bad, and had lately run away. I talked with her till her anger appeared to be abated, and she concluded her punishment with flinging the club she had in her hands at the poor creature's head, which made the blood run down on her garment. The slave continued with her hands tied behind her all night. They were untied this morning, and she spent the day in labour, which made me conclude she would be punished no more. But this evening I saw a large chain brought into the yard, with a ring at one end, just large enough to go round her neck. On this ring were fixed two pieces of iron about an inch wide and four inches long, which would come on each side of her face to prevent her eating. The chain was as large and heavy as an ox chain, and reached from her neck to the ground. The ring was fastened with a lock and key. The poor creature stood trembling while they were preparing to put the chain on her. The mistress' rage again rekindled at seeing her, and she began beating again, as the night before. I went to her again, and begged she would stop. She did, but so full of anger that she could hardly speak. When she had become a little calm, I asked her if she could not forgive her servant. I told her that her servant was very bad, but that she would be very good to forgive her. She

made me to understand that she would forgive her, because I had asked her; but she would not have her servant to think it was out of any favour to her. She told her slave that she forgave her, because I requested it. The slave came, knelt and kissed my feet, and said, 'Mercy, madam—mercy, madam,' meaning Thank you, madam. I could scarcely forbear weeping at her gratitude. The mistress promised me the chain should not be put on her, and ordered it carried away. I have felt very happy this evening, that this poor slave can lie down and sleep without that heavy chain. How happy are the inhabitants of New-England, who witness no such scenes of cruelty, and where every servant has his freedom as well as his master.[1] But O, my dear sisters, how much more wretched is the spiritual than the temporal state of these slaves! They have none to tell them of their danger, none to lead them to that Saviour who is equally the friend of the slave and the master (101–2).

The missionaries were allowed to minister to the English soldiers on the island, but knew that they would not be permitted to evangelize the slave population. More than ever they felt the frustration of being unable to begin the work to which they felt called. In the same letter to her sisters Ann wrote:

We long to get to the place where we shall spend the remainder of our lives in instructing the heathen. I want one of you with me very much, as I am entirely alone. I wish it was possible for one of you to come. A voyage from America here looks trifling to what it did when I was in America. I expect to take one or two more voyages before we are settled. How happy should I feel to spend one evening at home, and give you an account of the scenes through which we have passed. But that happiness I

do not expect to enjoy. I often look at death with very animating feelings. Then I hope to meet all my friends, to be no more separated (102–3).

The small missionary group—the Judsons, Samuel Newell and Luther Rice—were now themselves to be separated. Samuel Newell, the only Congregationalist of the four, decided to try to join his fellow-Congregationalists, the Notts and Hall. They were thought to have left India for Ceylon and in February 1813 Newell left for that island. When Luther Rice suffered a breakdown in health, it was decided in March 1813 that he should return to America where he could attempt to rally the Baptists behind the missionary cause. Ann wrote:

> [*March*] *13*. Brother Rice has just left us, and taken passage for America. Mr. J. and I are now entirely alone—not one remaining friend in this part of the world. The scenes through which we pass are calculated to remind us, that this world is not our home, and that we are fast verging towards the grave (99).

Rice proved himself to be a most able advocate of foreign missions and worked tirelessly back in America to raise support for the Judsons and those Baptist missionaries who joined them.

By now, the uncertainty as to the future of their mission was beginning to tell on both Ann and Adoniram. It was a year and a quarter since they had left home with such high hopes and expectations. Eventually it was decided that they would try to start a mission at Penang (Prince of Wales' Island, situated on the coast of Malacca, see page 74). No passage to that island could be obtained from the Isle of France, so they sailed for Madras in May 1813 in the hope of picking up a passage from there to Penang.

The following diary extract shows a continuing trust that the Lord would overrule:

May 6. Have been distressed for some days, on account of the gloomy prospect before us. We have engaged a passage to Madras, and expect soon to embark, not knowing what will befall us there. We shall probably meet with great difficulties and trials; and we know not to what part of the world we shall have next to direct our course. Every thing respecting our little mission is involved in uncertainty. I find it hard to live by faith, and confide entirely in God, when the way is dark before me. But if the way were plain and easy, where would be the room for confidence in God? (103).

Before they left the Isle of France, Ann took time to visit the grave where her childhood friend had been buried:

April 10. Have just returned from Harriet's grave—not able to visit it before, on account of the distance. The visit revived many painful, solemn feelings. But a little while ago, she was with us on board ship, and joined us daily in prayer and praise. Now her body is crumbling to dust, in a land of strangers, and her immortal spirit has doubtless joined the company of holy spirits around the throne, where she can sing in much more exalted strains, than when a prisoner here below. I was struck on beholding a large cross in the centre of the cemetery, higher than any of the grave-stones. This reminded me of the triumph of the cross over death and the grave, a triumph of which every saint will at last partake, and be crowned with eternal life (100).

Grief for Harriet was mixed, no doubt, with fear for herself. By now, Ann was expecting a baby. Where it would be born was, as yet, unknown.

Burma in the early 19th century

7

To the Golden Kingdom (1813)

When the American Board commissioned the departing missionaries, it was to the Burman Empire that they were directed—if possible. Adoniram had become gripped with a vision for mission to Asia through reading a sermon entitled 'The Star in the East' by Dr Claudius Buchanan. This had concentrated on the progress, to date, of the gospel in India. But he then found a book entitled *An Account of an Embassy to the Kingdom of Ava* by Michael Symes, a British army officer who had spent time in Burma. From that time on Adoniram was fascinated by this nation.

The Burman Empire lay between India and China, isolated by mountains on the borders. It was effectively a dictatorship, with absolute power exerted by the king. Symes gave the impression that there was a measure of toleration, but this was misleading. Roman Catholicism was tolerated among the Portuguese inhabitants, but in the recent past a Burmese man had been tortured nearly to death for converting to Christianity. The religion of Burma was Buddhism, a religion which

arose in the sixth century BC with the enlightenment of Gautama, the Buddha. He taught that all appearance is characterized by *dukkha* (transience), that there is not really such a thing as the soul and no eternal God. Thus the motivation which compelled the Judsons is described bluntly in the *Memoir:*

> The religion of Burmah, then, is, in effect, *atheism*; and the highest reward of piety, the object of earnest desire and unwearied pursuit, is annihilation. How wretched a system is this; how devoid of adequate motives to virtue; and how vacant of consolation! (122).

The British Baptists had directed their efforts first to India. William Carey and John Thomas had arrived in Bengal in 1793 and had managed to establish an extensive mission station at Serampore, twelve miles or so from Calcutta. They faced opposition from the British East India Company. When two new British Baptist missionaries were deported in 1806 one of them, James Chater, was sent to Burma to explore the possibility of a mission there. Two more missionaries arrived. One died; the other soon left. Chater stayed for four years and made a preliminary translation of the Gospel of Matthew into Burmese. When he appealed for reinforcements in 1807, William Carey's son Felix arrived in Burma and set himself to learn the language. He revised Chater's translation of the Gospel of Matthew and had a printing-press set up at Ava. In 1811 Felix married a woman of Portuguese extraction who had been born in Burma, and who was immersed in the language and customs. They set up home in Rangoon, and Felix continued language work. Chater left in 1812 and went on to found a mission in Ceylon.

Despite this start, the government was implacably opposed to any mission to convert the inhabitants from the Buddhist religion. Felix

was able to operate more or less unhindered because of his marriage to a 'local' and because his pioneer efforts were directed at language work rather than direct evangelization of the inhabitants. Burma had been very much on William Carey's missionary agenda, being made the special subject of prayer at Friday night prayer meetings at Serampore. But at the time of the arrival of the American missionaries in India, the door to Burma seemed firmly closed. The arrival of more missionaries might well compromise the work and safety of Felix Carey, and their own prospects would be perilous, to say the least. On 19 September 1812, Ann wrote from Calcutta:

> We had almost concluded to go to the Burman empire, when we heard there were fresh difficulties existing between the English and the Burman government. If these difficulties are settled, I think it probable we shall go there. It presents a very extensive field for usefulness, containing seventeen millions of inhabitants:—and the Scriptures have never been translated into their language. This circumstance is a very strong inducement to Mr. Judson to go there, as there is no other place where he could be equally useful in translating. But our privations and dangers would be great. There are no bread, potatoes, butter, and very little animal food. The natives live principally on rice and fish. I should have no society at all except Mr. J. for there is not an English female in all Rangoon. But I could easily give up these comforts, if the government was such as to secure safety to its subjects.

But where our lives would depend on the caprice of a monarch, or those who have the power of life and death, we could never feel safe, unless we always had strong faith in God. Notwithstanding these difficulties, we are perfectly willing to go, if Providence opens the way. Mr. Judson has written to Mr. Chater, at Ceylon,

to get all the information respecting that place he can. Felix
Carey has lately arrived from Rangoon, and wishes us to return
with him; he is entirely alone, there being no other missionary
in all Burmah (76–7).

All (except Felix Carey) had joined to advise against going to Burma
at the present time:

> Chater had repeated that in Burma they would be under
> both a king and local governors who were absolute despots
> and that governmental corruption was unbelievable.—And the
> laws were the bloodiest on earth: the commonest punishments
> were beheading, crucifixion, and 'pouring melted lead in small
> quantities down the throat,' and these were inflicted for such
> minor offences as chewing opium or drinking spirits.[1]

Harriet Newell had written in her journal in July 1812:

> We cannot feel that we are called in providence to Burmah.
> Every account we have from that savage, barbarous nation,
> confirms us in our opinion, that the way is not prepared for the
> spread of the Gospel there.[2]

Providence, however, intervened. When the Judsons returned
to Madras in June 1813, they were unable to find a ship bound for
Penang. They were in hourly expectation of an order to deport them
to England. Only one ship was due to sail anywhere and that ship
was bound for Rangoon, Burma. All their friends and acquaintances
at Madras urged them to avoid Burma at all costs, saying it would be
better to wait in England for another field to open up. But Adoniram
wrote:

... though dissuaded by all our friends at Madras, we commended ourselves to the care of God, and embarked on the 22nd of June. It was a crazy old vessel. The captain was the only person on board that could speak our language, and we had no other apartment than what was made by canvas.[3]

Ann commented in her diary:

June 20 [*1813*]. We have at last concluded, in our distress, to go to Rangoon, as there is no vessel about to sail for any other place, ere it will be too late to escape a second arrest. O, our heavenly Father, direct us aright! Where will thou have us go? What wilt thou have us do? Our only hope is in thee, and to thee alone we look for protection. O, let this mission yet live before thee, notwithstanding all opposition, and be instrumental of winning souls to Jesus in some heathen land. It is our present purpose to make Rangoon our final residence, if we find it practicable to live in such a place; otherwise, to go thence to Penang, or some of the Malay islands. But I most sincerely hope that we shall be able to remain at Rangoon, among the Burmans, a people who have never heard the sound of the Gospel, or read, in their own language, of the love of Christ... We cannot expect to do much, in such a rough, uncultivated field; yet if we may be instrumental in removing some of the rubbish, and preparing the way for others, it will be a sufficient reward. I have been accustomed to view this field of labour, with dread and terror; but now I feel perfectly willing to make it my home the rest of my life. I even feel a degree of pleasure, in the thought of living beyond the temptations peculiar to European settlements in the East. Our hearts will perhaps be more entirely devoted to our work, and the care of our own souls. Tomorrow we expect to leave this

place [Madras], and the few friends we have found here. Adieu
to polished, refined Christian society. Our lot is not cast among
you, but among pagans, among barbarians, whose tender mercies
are cruel (105–6).

Thus Ann and Adoniram Judson left for the 'Golden Kingdom'.
The voyage to Rangoon from Madras was a miserable one. They had
employed a European servant to accompany them on the journey,
but they had barely set foot on board ship when this woman, robust
enough in appearance, suddenly dropped dead. Ann herself became
dangerously ill, and Adoniram at one point almost resigned himself to
losing her. The journey was perilous, the ship unseaworthy. Like Harriet
before her, Ann gave birth on the journey. The baby was still born.

Just over three weeks after leaving Madras, the *Georgiana* made
her way up the Rangoon river. All the prospects before them seemed
utterly unattractive. Felix Carey described Rangoon as about one and
a half miles in length, a mile in breadth, thinly populated and in the
vicinity of jungle where deer, tigers and elephants roamed. The town
was infested with flies, rats and other vermin. Houses were raised above
the ground, and rubbish thrown underneath. An English traveller at
that time concurred. He described Rangoon as:

> A miserable, dirty town, containing 8,000 or 10,000 inhabitants,
> the houses being built with bamboo and teak planks, with
> thatched roofs—almost without drainage, and intersected by
> muddy creeks, through which the tide flowed at high water. It
> had altogether a mean, uninviting appearance...[4]

A few of the inhabitants were of Portuguese extraction, and they
had two or three Roman Catholic priests to minister to them. The

only 'gold' perceptible in this centre of the 'Golden Kingdom' was the flashing roof of the enormous Shwe Dagon Pagoda, one of the wonders of the world, a four-hundred-foot-high structure built over a sacred relic consisting of eight of the hairs of Buddha himself.

Ann described their arrival to her parents as follows in a letter dated 30 July 1813:

> We felt very gloomy and dejected the first night we arrived, in view of our prospects; but we were enabled to lean on God, and to feel that he was able to support us under the most discouraging circumstances. The next morning I prepared to go on shore, but hardly knew how I should get to Mr. Carey's house, as there was no method of conveyance, except a horse, while I was unable to ride. It was, however, concluded that I should be carried in an armed chair; consequently when I landed, one was provided, through which were put two bamboos, and four of the natives took me on their shoulders. When they had carried me a little way into the town, they set me down under a shade, when great numbers of the natives gathered around, as they had seldom seen an English female. Being sick and weak, I held my head down, which induced many of the native females to come very near, and look under my bonnet. At this I looked up and smiled, at which they set up a loud laugh. They again took me up to carry, and the multitude of natives gave a shout, which much diverted us. They next carried me to a place they call the custom-house. It was a small open shed, in which were seated on mats several natives, who were the custom-house officers. After searching Mr. Judson very closely, they asked liberty for a native female to search me, to which I readily consented. I was then brought to the mission-house, where I have entirely recovered my health (126).

This mission house had been built by the British missionary Chater

...in a pleasant rural spot, almost half a mile from the walls of the town. The house was built of teak wood, and was large and convenient for that climate... Connected with it were gardens inclosed, containing about two acres of ground, and full of fruit trees... (125–6).

Lest this give too idyllic an impression Wayland pointed out that it was also situated near the city rubbish heap, the public execution ground and the place for burning the dead.[5] But the building of this mission house had represented a huge cost in time, effort and finance. The Judsons were spared all of this and were able to move straight in. The mission house at this time was inhabited by Felix Carey, his Portuguese wife and small son; another baby would soon be born.

At the time of the Judsons' arrival Felix had been summoned to the capital, Ava, by the king in order to vaccinate[6] members of the royal family. Mrs Carey knew little English, but the Judsons were made comfortable and were free to begin language study.

A week after their arrival, Ann had sufficiently recovered her spirits to be able to view their prospects with a measure of optimism:

July 22. It is now a week since we arrived here. My health is quite restored, and I feel much more contented and happy, than I ever expected to be in such a situation. I think I do enjoy the promises of God, in a higher degree than ever before, and have attained more true peace of mind and trust in the Saviour. When I look back to my late situation, in that wretched old vessel, without any accommodations—scarcely the necessaries of life—no

physician—no female attendants—so weak, that I could not move, I hope that I am deeply sensible of the kind care of my heavenly Father, in carrying me safely through the peculiar dangers of the voyage, and giving me once more a resting place on land. Still, were it not for the support we derive from the Gospel of Jesus, we should be ready to sink down in despondency, in view of the dark and gloomy scenes around us. But when we recollect that Jesus has commanded his disciples to carry the Gospel to the heathen, and promised to be with them to the end of the world; that God has promised to give the heathen to his Son for an inheritance, we are encouraged to make a beginning, though in the midst of discouragement, and leave it to him to grant success, in his own time and way. I find here no dear female friends, with whom I can unite in social prayer, nor even one with whom I can converse. I have, indeed, no society at all, but that of Mr. J.; yet I feel happy in thinking, that I give up this source of pleasure, as well as most others, for the sake of the poor heathen ... O if it may please the dear Redeemer to make me instrumental of leading some of the females of Burmah to a saving acquaintance with him, my great object would be accomplished, my highest desires gratified: I shall rejoice to have relinquished my comforts, my country, and my home (127–8).

And a month later, the following prayer is recorded in her memoir:

When, blessed Lord, wilt thou visit Burmah, and take up thine abode in the hearts of these idolaters? When wilt thou be pleased to gratify those desires and longings, which thou hast thyself excited in our hearts? When shall cruel, idolatrous, avaricious Burmah know, that thou art the God of the whole earth, and

alone deservest the homage and adoration of all creatures? Hasten it, Lord, in thine own time (130).

8

Years of toil (1813–1815)

In July 1813, Ann and Adoniram arrived in what was to be their place of ministry for the rest of their lives. Having left New England on 18 February 1812, they had endured nearly a year and a half of travel, raised hopes, uncertainty and disappointment. Now they lost no time in beginning language study, the indispensable foundation for future work. They had not anticipated just how difficult this would be. Ann commented on 15 August 1813:

> I have begun to study the language. Find it very hard and difficult, having none of the usual helps in acquiring a language, except a small part of a grammar, and six chapters of St. Matthew's Gospel by Mr. Carey, now at Ava (129).

They engaged a Hindu teacher and had to begin by simply pointing at objects and learning the names—a frustrating method which yielded slow returns. They then began trying to study the written language.

In a letter written in 1816 Adoniram revealed the frustrations and
difficulty this entailed:

> I just now begin to see my way forward in this language, and
> hope that two or three years more will make it somewhat familiar;
> but I have met with difficulties that I had no idea of before I
> entered on the work. For a European or American to acquire a
> living oriental language, root and branch, and make it his own,
> is quite a different thing from his acquiring a cognate language
> of the west, or any of the dead languages, as they are studied
> in the schools … When … we take up a language spoken by a
> people on the other side of the earth, whose very thoughts run in
> channels diverse from ours, and whose modes of expression are
> consequently all new and uncouth; when we find the letters and
> words all totally destitute of the least resemblance to any language
> we had ever met with, and these words not fairly divided, and
> distinguished, as in western writing, by breaks, and points, and
> capitals, but run together in one continuous line, a sentence or
> paragraph seeming to the eye but one long word; when, instead
> of clear characters on paper, we find only obscure scratches on
> dried palm leaves strung together, and called a book; when we
> have no dictionary, and no interpreter to explain a single word,
> and must get something of the language, before we can avail
> ourselves of the assistance of a native teacher … It unavoidably
> takes several years to acquire such a language, in order to converse
> and write intelligibly on the great truths of the Gospel. Dr. Carey
> once told me, that after he had been some years in Bengal and
> thought he was doing very well, in conversing and preaching
> with the natives, they (as he was afterwards convinced) knew
> not what he was about. A young Missionary, who expects to pick

up the language in a year or two, will probably find that he has not counted the cost (149–50).

Patience paid dividends. Adoniram was convinced that there was no point in beginning direct evangelistic work until the language had been mastered and at least a major part of the Scriptures translated. He saw himself as laying the foundation upon which others could build. And so, month after month, he kept up the punishing twelve-hour-a-day study routine, until his eyesight failed and his stamina broke under the strain.

The Judsons were soon left alone as missionaries in Burma. Felix Carey had gained favour with the local people in Rangoon by carrying out vaccinations; when the Judsons arrived in Rangoon he had been in Ava vaccinating the children of the king. When he returned to Rangoon later in 1813 he was impressed by the Judsons. He wrote to his father, William Carey, 'They are just cut out for this mission. I thought so, as soon as I first met them. In six months Mr. Judson has a splendid grasp of the language, and is the very colleague I wanted.'[1] Felix had, however, accepted various commissions from the Burmese government. In 1814 he planned to move to Ava, where perhaps he hoped that he could set up a mission as well as work for the king. He believed that the mission would ultimately benefit if he continued in the king's favour through medical and diplomatic work. But on 15 November 1815 he resigned from the mission at Serampore which had sent him out to Burma. By this time he had suffered the appalling loss of his wife, two children and all his possessions in a boat accident on the way up to Ava in August 1814. This tragedy further unsettled a man who was of an insecure temperament and prone to depression.[2]

Ann and Adoniram were left in possession of the mission house, alone in Rangoon. They had established a daily routine, which Ann described as follows:

> As it respects ourselves, we are busily employed all day long. I can assure you that we find much pleasure in our employment. Could you look into a large open room, which we call a verandah, you would see Mr. Judson bent over his table, covered with Burman books, with his teacher at his side, a venerable looking man in his sixtieth year, with a cloth wrapped round his middle, and a handkerchief round his head. They talk and chatter all day long, with hardly any cessation.

> My mornings are busily employed in giving directions to the servants—providing food for the family, etc. At ten my teacher comes, when, were you present, you might see me in an inner room, at one side of my study table, and my teacher the other, reading Burman, writing, talking, etc. I have many more interruptions than Mr. Judson, as I have the entire management of the family. This I took upon myself, for the sake of Mr. Judson's attending more closely to the study of the language; yet I have found by a year's experience, that it was the most direct way I could have taken to acquire the language; as I am frequently obliged to speak Burman all day. I can talk and understand others better than Mr. Judson, though he knows more about the nature and construction of the language (137–8).

Adoniram was indeed mastering the construction of the language with enormous care. He was acutely aware of his responsibility as the one who would lay a foundation upon which succeeding missionaries could build. From the beginning he aimed to produce a grammar and

dictionary, and was making word-lists and notes to begin this great task. Not only was he working on the Burmese language but, realizing that this language lacked ethical and abstract terminology, he worked in parallel on the Pali language. This was used in the Buddhist sacred writings and by the Buddhist priests.

They were also careful to try to establish good relations with the ruler of Rangoon. In December 1813 Ann had been introduced to the wife of the viceroy and described this meeting:

> *Dec. 11.* Today, for the first time, I have visited the wife of the viceroy. I was introduced to her by a French lady who has frequently visited her. When we first arrived at the government house, she was not up, consequently we had to wait some time. But the inferior wives of the viceroy diverted us much by their curiosity, in minutely examining every thing we had on, and by trying on our gloves and bonnets, etc. At last her highness made her appearance, dressed richly in the Burman fashion with a long silver pipe in her mouth, smoking. At her appearance, all the other wives took their seats at a respectful distance, and sat in a crouching posture, without speaking. She received me very politely, took me by the hand, seated me upon a mat, and herself by me. She excused herself for not coming in sooner, saying she was unwell. One of the women brought her a bunch of flowers, of which she took several and ornamented my cap. She was very inquisitive whether I had a husband and children, whether I was my husband's first wife—meaning by this, whether I was the highest among them, supposing that Mr. Judson, like the Burmans, had many wives; and whether I intended tarrying long in the country.

When the viceroy came in, I really trembled; for I never before beheld such a savage looking creature. His long robe, and enormous spear, not a little increased my dread. He spoke to me, however, very condescendingly, and asked if I would drink some rum or wine. When I arose to go, her highness again took my hand, told me she was happy to see me, that I must come to see her every day. She led me to the door; I made my *salam*, and departed. My only object in visiting her was, that if we should get into any difficulty with the Burmans, I could have access to her, when perhaps it would not be possible for Mr. Judson to have an audience with the viceroy (135–6).

By the August of the following year she wrote:

A new viceroy has lately arrived, who is much beloved and respected by the people. He visited us soon after his arrival, and told us that we must come to the government house very often. We have been once or twice since, and were treated with much more familiarity and respect than are natives of the country (138).

The Judsons found the brutality of Burmese law hard to witness. Ann wrote in January 1815:

In consequence of the robbery committed a few days ago, the viceroy ordered seven thieves to be executed … They were tied up by the hands and feet, and then cut open, and left with their bowels hanging out. They are to remain a spectacle to others for three days, and then be buried.[3]

Every opportunity was taken in private conversation to try to introduce the gospel:

We often converse with our teachers and servants on the subject of our coming to this country, and tell them if they die in their present state they will surely be lost. But they say, 'Our religion is good for us, yours for you.' But we are far from being discouraged. We are sensible that the hearts of the heathen, as well as those of Christians, are in the hands of God, and in his own time he will turn them unto him (138).

Ann's journal shows that she continued to exercise a rigorous discipline of private self-examination, but also that she had to battle against intense and real homesickness:

> [*Aug.*] *28* [*1813*]. I fear that I have declined in religion the past week. Nothing do I dread so much as becoming cold and worldly-minded, and losing the life of religion in the soul. Though I have but few temptations, I find that the innate depravity of my heart is constantly showing itself, in some way or other. I find it is just as necessary to watch and pray, and guard against easily besetting sins, in this heathen land, as in any other situation. O for a more holy heart, more fervent love to God, and more ardent longings for the promotion of his cause!
>
> Have been writing letters this week to my dear friends in America. Found that a recollection of former enjoyments, in my own native country, made my situation here appear less tolerable. The thought that I had parents, sisters and beloved friends, still in existence, and at such a distance, that it was impossible to obtain a look, or exchange a word, was truly painful. While they are still in possession of the comforts I once enjoyed, I am an exile from my country, and my father's house, deprived of all society, and every friend, but one, and with scarcely the necessaries of

life. These privations would not be endured with patience, in any other cause, but that in which we are engaged (131).

A year after she wrote this, in September 1814, letters finally arrived from her sister. Ann was overjoyed, and responded:

Two long years and a half had elapsed since we left our native country without hearing one word from any of our American friends. Thirteen months of this time have been spent in the cruel, avaricious, benighted country of Burmah, without a single Christian friend or female companion of any sort.[4]

Quite why she did not count Mrs Carey (who had been with them at the mission house until only a few weeks earlier) as a female companion is unclear. Felix's wife was a Roman Catholic, of Portuguese birth. Perhaps the language was a barrier; perhaps she and Ann found little common ground. Or maybe Ann was merely indulging in a bit of exaggeration to highlight the loneliness she found so hard to bear.

The motivation for perseverance is made clear in a letter she wrote to Samuel Newell at around this time:

As it respects our temporal privations, use has made them familiar and easy to be borne; they are of short duration, and when brought in competition with the worth of immortal souls, sink into nothing. We have no society, no dear Christian friends, and with the exception of two or three sea captains, who now and then call on us, we never see a European face. When we feel a disposition to sigh for the enjoyments of our native country, we turn our eyes on the miserable objects around. We behold some of them labouring hard for a scanty subsistence, oppressed

by an avaricious government, which is ever ready to seize what industry has hardly earned. We behold others sick and diseased, daily begging the few grains of rice, which, when obtained, are scarcely sufficient to protract their wretched existence, and with no other habitation to cover them from the burning sun or chilly rains, than that which a small piece of cloth raised on four bamboos, under the shade of a tree, can afford. While we behold these scenes, we feel that we have all the comforts, and in comparison even the luxuries of life. We feel that our temporal cup of blessings is full and runneth over. But is our temporal lot so much superior to theirs? O how infinitely superior are our spiritual blessings! While they vainly imagine to purchase promotion in another state of existence, by strictly worshipping their idols, and building pagodas, our hopes of future happiness are fixed on the Lamb of God, who taketh away the sin of the world. When we have a realizing sense of these things, my dear brother, we forget our native country and former enjoyments, feel contented and happy with our lot, with but one wish remaining—that of being instrumental of leading these Burmans to partake of the same source of happiness with ourselves.

Our progress in the language is slow, as it is peculiarly hard of acquisition. We can, however, read, write, and converse with tolerable ease; and frequently spend whole evenings very pleasantly in conversing with our Burman friends. We have been very fortunate in procuring good instructors. Mr. Judson's teacher is a very learned man, was formerly a priest, and resided at court. He has a thorough knowledge of the grammatical construction of the language; likewise of the Pali, the learned language of the Burmans (138–9).

At the beginning of 1815[5] Ann fell seriously ill, and there were no doctors in Rangoon. Adoniram wanted to accompany her to Madras to consult with a doctor, but she would not hear of his leaving his studies. She sailed alone in January, and returned in April, bringing back a little seven-year-old orphan girl to join the family. Emily Van Someren would live with the Judsons for seven years, before returning to Madras in 1822. Very little is said of her.

At last, on 5 September 1815, letters arrived from America bringing the first news regarding their support since Luther Rice had left them two long years before. The Baptists of New England had rallied round the cause of mission in a remarkable way. Local societies had been formed for the support of the Judsons. In May 1814 a national missionary society had been formed. The Judsons and Rice were adopted as Baptist missionaries, Rice initially being commissioned to continue the work of setting up new local branches. Moreover a printer, George Hough, had been sent out to Burma in order to support Adoniram by printing anything he was able to produce in Burmese. George and his wife Phebe were getting ready to leave at the time. This was an enormous encouragement to Ann and Adoniram.

On 11 September 1815, Ann gave birth to a healthy baby boy, whom they named Roger Williams Judson (in honour of the great American Baptist, Roger Williams). They were overjoyed. Their elation increased when just three weeks later Adoniram had the most encouraging conversation yet with his teacher. At last progress was being made. Adoniram continued his punishing schedule of language work, more convinced than ever that the gospel would ultimately bear fruit in this seemingly impenetrable culture. And meanwhile baby Roger brought his parents pure joy. Ann wrote to her parents on 26 September:

After an absence of three months, I safely arrived at Rangoon, where I found Mr. Judson well, and labouring hard, though entirely alone. My health continued to mend, and on the 11th of September, I was made the happy mother of a little son. I had no physician or assistant whatever excepting Mr. Judson. Since the birth of our little son my health has been much better than for two years before. I feel now almost in a new state of existence. Our hands are full, and though our prospects in regard to the immediate conversion of the Burmans are dark, yet our trust in God is strong, and our hopes animating (144).

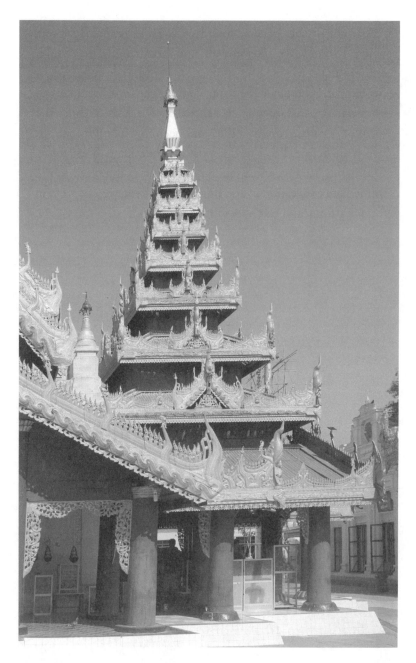

Buddhist temple in Burma

9

'This heavy affliction' (1816)

By the end of 1815 both Adoniram and Ann felt fluent in everyday conversation, and Adoniram had made solid progress in mastering the construction of the language. The major obstacle to the success of their mission was evidently going to be the great chasm, in terms of concepts and beliefs, between themselves and those whose conversion they sought. As Ann wrote to her sisters in December 1815:

> In regard to the language, which sister A. wishes 'to hear how it sounds,' we feel quite at home, and can converse with ease on common subjects. We find the subject of religion by far the most difficult, on account of the want of religious terms in their language. They have not the least idea of a God who is eternal—without beginning or end. All their deities have been through the several grades of creatures, from a fowl to a deity. When their deities take heaven, as they express it, they cease to exist, which, according to their ideas, is the highest state of perfection. It is now two thousand years since Gaudama, their last deity,

entered on his state of perfection; and though he now ceases to exist, they still worship a hair of his head, which is enshrined in an enormous pagoda, to which the Burmans go every eighth day. They know of no other atonement for sin, than offerings to their priests and their pagodas. You cannot imagine how very difficult it is to give them any idea of the true God and the way of salvation by Christ, since their present ideas of deity are so very low.

Mr. Judson has obtained a tolerable knowledge of the construction of the language, and only needs time and practice to make it perfectly familiar. I can read and write, but am far behind Mr. J. in this part, though in conversation I am his equal. Doubtless you expect by this time, that some of the Burmans have embraced the Christian religion, or at least, are seriously inquiring respecting it. Our hopes have frequently been raised by the serious and candid attention of some, but have as frequently sunk again by beholding their almost total indifference … (146).

She went on to describe the effect in the town of a change of viceroy, and then gives some hint as to the continuing battle with longing for home:

The town just now is all in confusion. The present viceroy is recalled by the king, and the former viceroy is again to take the government of Rangoon. The present viceroy has been here only a year and three months; he is much beloved by the people, ten thousand of whom will go with him. We have had a very peaceable, comfortable time during his administration; the town was in a flourishing state; robberies very seldom, on account of the effectual means he has taken to suppress them, and we

strongly hoped he would be permitted to continue here for some
time. The present viceroy and his wife are nearly related to the
king. They have a daughter fifteen years old, who on her arrival
at Ava is to be presented to the prince regent. She is a sensible,
smart, satirical girl; with a mind as capable of improvement
as any young lady in America. She and her mother have ever
treated me with marked attention. I went to take leave of them
two or three days ago, and when I entered the room where they
receive company, finding they were not present, I took my seat
with the women who had assembled to pay their respects, and
which is two or three steps lower than where the viceroy's family
sit. When the wife and daughter came in, they immediately told
me to take my place with them, for it was not fitting that the
wife of a priest should sit there. When I came away, her ladyship
presented me with a string of coral, which is the second she has
given me since her residence here.

O how I long to visit Bradford! and spend a few evenings by
your firesides, in telling you what I have seen and heard. Alas!
we have no fireside, no social circle; we are still alone in this
miserable country, surrounded by thousands who are ignorant of
the true God and only way of salvation by Jesus Christ ... (148).

During the early part of 1816 Adoniram and Ann continued to
be encouraged in the work and enthralled with the new addition to
their family. On 26 September 1815, a couple of weeks after the birth
of their son Roger, Ann had written to her mother:

I know, my dear mother, you long very much to see my little
boy. I wish you were here to see him. He is a little sprightly
boy, and already begins to be very playful. We hope his life may

be preserved and his heart sanctified, that he may become a Missionary among the Burmans (145).

Little Roger delighted others as well. He was even admired by the new viceroy! When March came round, the baby began suffering night fevers. Ann was anxious, and things were made worse by Adoniram's health giving way at this time. He suffered severe eye-strain and headaches as a result of his unremitting study. He managed to complete a tract in the Burmese language summarizing the main truths of Christianity, but then was increasingly disabled through weakness and pain. Work was severely curtailed, and he wondered whether his usefulness had come to an end. The worst blow of all came in May, as Ann wrote to her parents:

> Little did I think when I wrote you last, that my next letter would be filled with the melancholy subject on which I must now write. Death, regardless of our lonely situation, has entered our dwelling, and made one of the happiest families wretched. Our little Roger Williams, our only little darling boy, was three days ago laid in the silent grave. Eight months we enjoyed the precious little gift, in which time he had so completely entwined himself around his parents' hearts, that his existence seemed necessary to their own. But God has taught us by afflictions, what we would not learn by mercies—that our hearts are his exclusive property, and whatever rival intrudes, he will tear it away.
>
> As I feel incapable of writing on any other subject, I will give you the particulars of his little probation, and the last painful scene which has rent our hearts.

He was a remarkably pleasant child—never cried except when in pain, and, what we often observed to each other was the most singular, he never, during his little existence, manifested the least anger or resentment at any thing. This was not owing to the want of intellect, for his tender feelings of sensibility were very conspicuous. Whenever I or his father passed his cradle without taking him, he would follow us with his eyes to the door, when they would fill with tears, and his countenance so expressive of grief, though perfectly silent, that it would force us back to him, which would cause his little heart to be as joyful as it had been sorrowful. He would lie hours on his papa's study table, or by the side of his chair on the floor, if he could only see his face. When we had finished study or the business of the day, it was our exercise and amusement to carry him round the house or garden, and though we were alone, we felt not our solitude when he was with us. For two months before he died, I observed with much anxiety, that he had violent fits of perspiration every night, and a slight degree of fever. But as he appeared well through the day, and had a good appetite for his food, and continued to grow fleshy, I strongly hoped it would wear off, and terminate in the cutting of his teeth. But alas! all our hopes were blasted. Tuesday morning when I took him from his cradle, he appeared as well as usual; but not long after, he was taken with a violent coughing, which continued without cessation for half an hour. This brought on a fever, which continued strong through the day and night; but Wednesday morning it abated, and he slept quietly through the day, and took his food with as good an appetite as usual. Thursday his cough returned, and with it the fever, which again much alarmed us, and we sent for a Portuguese priest, (the only person who knows any thing about medicine in the place) who gave him a little rhubarb and gascoign powder. But nothing

appeared to affect the distress in his throat, which was the cause of his coughing, and made him breathe so hard that every breath could be heard some way. Friday night I sat by him till two o'clock, when being much fatigued, I retired, and Mr. Judson took him. The little creature drank his milk with much eagerness, (he was weaned) and Mr. Judson thought he was refreshed and would go to sleep. He laid him in his cradle,—he slept with ease for half an hour, when his breath stopped without a struggle, and he was gone! Thus died our little Roger …

We buried him in the afternoon of the same day, in a little enclosure the other side of the garden. Forty or fifty Burmans and Portuguese followed with his afflicted parents, the last remains to the silent grave. All the Burmans who were acquainted with us endeavoured to sympathize with us, and console us under our loss. Our little Roger was the only legitimate child of foreign parents in the place, consequently he was quite a curiosity to the Burmans. But what shall I say about the improvement we are to make of this heavy affliction? We do not feel a disposition to murmur, or to enquire of our Sovereign why he has done this. We wish, rather, to sit down submissively under the rod and bear the smart, till the end for which the affliction was sent shall be accomplished. Our hearts were bound up in this child; we felt he was an earthly all, our only source of innocent recreation in this heathen land. But God saw it was necessary to remind us of our error, and to strip us of our only little all. O may it not be in vain that he has done it. May we so improve it, that he will stay his hand, and say, 'It is enough' (151–3).

Baby Roger died on 4 May 1816, aged seven months and twenty-three days. On 7 May Adoniram wrote:

Our little comfort, our dear little Roger, has become insensible to our parental attentions and fond caresses ... his sweet face has become cold to our lips, and his little mind ... has ... fled—oh, where? ... Who supports and guides its trembling steps across the dark valley? There a parent's aid could not be extended. But we hope it had a more affectionate and abler guide. We hope that Jesus has repaired the ruins of the fall in regard to all little children. And who but thinks their departed children sweet and lovely beyond compare? Perhaps I am a novice in affliction. Had I lost a wife, I might not thus lament for a little child eight months old. Yet nothing but such a scene of bereavement and anguish as we have passed through can teach us to pity others in like circumstances. Nothing but experience can teach us what feelings agonize the soul of a parent when he puts his face to that of his dear, his only child, to ascertain whether there may not be one breath more; and when satisfied of the truth, when hope expires with life, he tries to raise the bursting aspiration: O Lord, receive the spirit!

Our little Roger died last Saturday morning. We looked at him through the day, and on the approach of night we laid him in the grave.[1]

On 18 May Ann wrote:

It is just a fortnight today, since our little boy died. We feel the anguish a little abated, and have returned to our study and employment; but when for a moment we realize what we once possessed, and our now bereaved state, the wound opens and bleeds afresh. Yet we would still say, 'Thy will be done.'

Two or three days ago the wife of the viceroy made us a visit
in all her state. She had heard of the death of the little white
child, as she called him, and came to pay a visit of condolence
… When she saw me after his death, she smote her breast, and
said, 'Why did you not send me word, that I might come to his
funeral?' I told her I did not think of any thing, my distress was
so great. She then tried to comfort us, and told us not to weep.
She was accompanied by all her officers of state and attendants,
all of which were about two hundred people. I gave her tea,
sweetmeats, and cakes, with which she appeared much pleased.
O that she might become a real disciple of Jesus! (153–4).

The viceroy's wife was determined to try to help. She sent an elephant
to convey Ann and Adoniram on an excursion into the countryside
so that 'their minds might become cool'. A procession of hundreds
of retainers accompanied five or six elephants which carried the VIPs
in richly decorated howdahs. After a ride of about four miles there
was a picnic in one of the viceroy's gardens. Ann wrote afterwards:

We returned in the evening, fatigued with riding on the elephant,
delighted with the view of the country and the hospitality of
the Burmans, and dejected and depressed with their superstition
and idolatry—their darkness and ignorance of the true God.[2]

The death of Roger was one of the hardest experiences Ann had
to endure. She suffered a lasting sadness, a wound that would ache
for the rest of her life. But she and Adoniram threw themselves once
more into the work to which they had devoted their lives. And soon
there would be the comfort of reinforcements to join them.

10

'Strange vicissitudes': seven months of suspense (1817–1818)

The period in 1816 after the death of baby Roger and before Adoniram recovered his health was a discouraging one. Ann commented: 'All is Egyptian darkness around us—not a glimpse of light ...' (154). She started a school for girls (eventually numbering between twenty and thirty) and worked on a catechism for children. She capitalized on opportunities to share the gospel with the mothers of the girls. Adoniram's health remained poor, but even during his illness he laboured on a Burmese dictionary to aid future missionaries.

Gradually exercise and a better diet led to recovery, but best of all was the news that George and Phebe Hough, with their two children, had arrived in Calcutta in April 1816. William Carey generously provided them with a printing-press and other equipment, and they arrived in Rangoon in October. George Hough wrote of his first impressions:

The few with whom Brother Judson has conversed since I
have been here, appear inaccessible to truth. They sit unaffected,
and go away unimpressed with what they have heard. They
are unconvinced by arguments, and unmoved by love; and the
conversion of a Burman, or even the excitement of a thought
towards the truth, must and will be a sovereign act of divine
power. We long to see that act of power displayed: even one
instance would fill us with joy (158).

George and Phebe moved into the mission house with Ann and
Adoniram, and soon printing was under way. Two tracts, one a summary
of Christian doctrine prepared by Adoniram, the other a children's
catechism by Ann, were printed (1,000 and 3,000 copies respectively).
Work commenced on setting up an edition of 800 copies of Judson's
translation of the Gospel of Matthew which he completed in May 1817.

A letter written by Adoniram at this time displays the long-term
vision which kept them going despite no visible success. He pointed
to other mission-fields where conversions had occurred only after
many years of preparatory labour:

If any ask what success I meet with among the natives—tell
them to look at Otaheite ... Tell them to look at Bengal ... If
they ask again what prospect of *ultimate* success is there—tell
them, as much as that there is an Almighty and faithful God,
who will perform his promises, and no more. If this does not
satisfy them, beg them to let me stay and make the attempt ...
And if we live some twenty or thirty years, they may hear from
us again ... (156–7).

Catechism in the Burmese language prepared by Ann Judson

He went on to say that Rangoon was a 'most wretched place' and yet if a ship arrived to take him anywhere in the world he chose, he would remain:

> This is an immense field; and, since the Serampore Missionaries have left it, it seems wholly thrown on the hands of the Americans. If we desert it, the blood of the Burmans will be required of us (157).

It was the long-term perspective which enabled Adoniram to persevere with the hard work of language study, and avoid the temptation to go straight for visible success. Hough commented soon after his arrival:

> Brother Judson has never yet been abroad to preach. He has applied himself constantly to the study of the language, with a view to the translation of the New Testament. We both concur in the opinion, that before preaching be undertaken, to any considerable degree, some portion of the Scriptures should be in circulation (158).

As the missionaries considered the prospect of commencing public preaching, they were all too aware that the position of the mission house was a real disadvantage. The Judsons had made an early attempt to move into Rangoon. This had come to nothing when their house burned down, and they had moved back to the mission. Adoniram commented in March 1817:

> Our present house [the mission house] is situated in the woods, away from any neighbours, and at a distance from any road. In this situation, we have no visitors, and no passing travellers, whom

we could invite to stop and hear of Christ. My attempts to go out and find auditors have always occasioned such a waste of time, and interruption of study, as would not often be indulged in or justified. We are very desirous of building a small house near the town, or some public road (162).

Even given the less than ideal position of the mission house, Ann was able to start a regular work among the women on Sundays. She describes this work to a friend:

How interested you would be, could you meet with my little society of females, on the Sabbath. Interested I say—yes, you would be interested, if it was only from this circumstance—that these poor idolaters enjoy the means of grace, and sit under the sound of the Gospel. I have generally fifteen or twenty. They are attentive while I read the Scriptures, and endeavour to teach them about God. One of them told me the other day, that she could not think of giving up a religion which her parents, grand-parents, etc. etc. had embraced, and accepting a new one of which they had never heard. I asked her if she wished to go to hell, because her progenitors had gone there. She replied, if, with all her offerings and good works on her head, (speaking in their idiom) she must go to hell, then let her go. I told her, if she went to hell after having heard of the Saviour, her very relations would contribute to torment and upbraid her, for her rejection of that Saviour of whom they had never heard, and that even she herself would regret her folly when it was too late. If I do, said she, I will then cry out to you to be my intercessor with your God, who will certainly not refuse you. Another told me that she did believe in Christ, and prayed to him every day. I asked her if she also believed in Gaudama, and prayed to him.

She replied, she worshipped them both. I have several times had
my hopes and expectations raised, by the apparent seriousness of
several females, as Mr. Judson has in regard to several men; but
their goodness was like the morning cloud and early dew, which
soon passeth away. Four or five children have committed the
catechism to memory, and often repeat it to each other (163–4).

Real encouragement was forthcoming sooner than Adoniram had
expected. In March 1817 he wrote, 'I have this day been visited by the
first inquirer after religion, that I have seen in Burmah' (160). Many
conversations had taken place, but this one was different. This visitor
had read the two tracts, and seemed genuinely concerned about what
he had read, and so had deliberately come to find out more. This
incident showed that the printing of literature was having its effect.
Other enquirers followed, also having read the tracts. In August 1817
Ann wrote:

Many have called at the mission house, to inquire more
particularly into the *new religion*. But we have frequently
observed in these inquirers, a fear lest others should discover their
inclination to inquire. Sometimes, when two or three intimate
friends have been seriously engaged in conversing on religious
subjects, if others, with whom they were not acquainted, called
at the same time, they would be silent, and take their leave. This
makes us feel the importance of trying to obtain the patronage
of government. In a few months, Mr. Judson will complete a
dictionary of the Burman language; after which he will, perhaps,
go up to Ava, the residence of the king (163).

It would be a further two years before the first baptism of a Burmese
national took place in July 1819. But the intervening years saw a severe

trial of Ann's faith and courage. This was occasioned by the decision of Adoniram to attempt to sail to Chittagong (see map on page 74), twelve or so days' sea-journey away in Bengal, to make contact with some Burmese-speaking Christians there. He hoped to persuade one of them to come back to Rangoon with him as a helper, and to break the impression that Christianity was only for Westerners. In December 1817 an opportunity for a round trip by sea arose and Adoniram took it up. It was thought that he would be away only a short time, but the ship ran into head winds, never reached Chittagong, and on trying to reach Madras encountered equally impossible currents. It took twelve weeks before the ship was able to land anywhere, by which time Adoniram was critically ill and food and water had given out. From Masulipatam he had to make a three-hundred-mile trip by land to Madras. After three months there, in July 1818, he managed to get a passage back to Rangoon. He had been away seven months. The only news received by Ann during that whole time was that the ship had not arrived at Chittagong, nor at Bengal. She wrote to her parents on 18 June:

> I am still, my dear parents, in the same lonely situation as when I last wrote, full of anxiety and suspense. I know not what conclusion to draw from the circumstance of receiving no intelligence from Mr. Judson. It is now six months since he left me, and not a single line has ever been received relative to the ship … I am trying to bear this state of uncertainty as a heavy affliction, a painful chastisement, from my heavenly Father, inflicted, no doubt, for wise and gracious purposes. Perhaps it is only a prelude to greater afflictions. Perhaps this is the school in which I am to be taught the rudiments of suffering, and to prepare for those heavy trials, which without these first few lessons, crush as soon as inflicted. I feel, however, a dreadful conflict; sometimes

inclined to complain of these dark dispensations of Providence, at others endeavouring to make this language my own: 'Though He slay me, yet I will trust in Him.' My female prayer meetings have been on the decline, ever since Mr. Hough's examination at the Court House.[1]

It was during Adoniram's absence that the mission at Rangoon nearly came to an end. George Hough was summoned before the local court and threatened with expulsion, and then cholera hit the city. Worst of all were rumours of a war with Britain, which would lead to a total sea blockade. The Houghs decided that it was not viable to remain in Burma. They determined to move back to Calcutta, where they could continue the printing work, and were adamant that Ann should come with them on what seemed likely to be the last ship to leave Rangoon. Ann was in an agony of indecision: loath to leave Rangoon, as the only place where Adoniram was likely to find her; loath to stay, as a blockade would keep him out as well as her in. She wrote to a friend as follows:

July 14. Alone, my dear friends, in this great house, without an individual, excepting my little girl and Burmans, I take my pen to relate the strange vicissitudes through which I have passed within a few days.

On the 5th of this month, I embarked with Mr. Hough and family for Bengal, having previously disposed of what I could not take with me. I had engaged Mr. Judson's teacher to accompany me, that in case of meeting him in Bengal, he could go on with his Burman studies. But the teacher, fearing the difficulties arising from his being a Burman, broke his engagement, and refused to go. My disinclination to proceed in the course commenced, and

had increased to such a degree, that I was on the point of giving up the voyage myself; but my passage was paid, my baggage on board, and I knew not how to separate myself from the rest of the mission family. The vessel, however, was several days in going down the river; and when on the point of putting out to sea, the captain and officers ascertained that she was in a dangerous state, in consequence of having been improperly loaded, and that she must be detained for a day or two at the place in which she lay. I immediately resolved on giving up the voyage, and returning to town. Accordingly the captain sent up a boat with me, and engaged to forward my baggage the next day. I reached town in the evening—spent the night at the house of the only remaining Englishman in the place, and today have come out to the mission-house, to the great joy of all the Burmans left on our premises. Mr. Hough and his family will proceed, and they kindly and affectionately urge my return. I know I am surrounded by dangers on every hand, and expect to see much anxiety and distress; but at present I am tranquil, and intend to make an effort to pursue my studies as formerly, and leave the event with God (174–5).

A few days later, on 4 August 1818, Adoniram returned. Ann's courage had been rewarded. The reunion was joyous. Adoniram's voyage had proved fruitless, but he determined to commence public preaching without further delay.

11

'A sovereign act of divine power': the first Burmese convert (1819)

After the seven-month ordeal, Adoniram arrived back in Rangoon on 4 August 1818, as we noted at the end of the previous chapter. Reinforcements arrived the next month when two young couples, the Colmans and the Wheelocks, arrived from America on 19 September. Initially, however, they only hindered the work. Almost immediately the two young men manifested signs of tuberculosis, and the mission house, now crowded, was transformed into a hospital. The pressure on space lessened after 1 November, when the Hough family left for Bengal. George Hough decided that he could continue the printing work there, and after the unpleasant experiences of that year he wanted to get his family out of Burma.

After some months James Colman showed marks of recovery, but it was obvious to everyone that Edward Wheelock was terminally ill. Or rather, it was obvious to everyone except his wife, who refused

to accept the hopelessness of his plight. A serious rift developed between Eliza and the rest of the missionaries. They wished to face up to the inevitable and prepare him for death; she became paranoid and suspected that they were out to harm her husband. She resented all interference and determined to remove her sick husband from Rangoon. This flew in the face of advice from all the others, who saw that the trip would kill him. The Wheelocks embarked for Bengal on 7 August 1819. During the voyage, Edward threw himself overboard and drowned.

However, all was not unrelieved gloom. It was during this miserable episode that real, tangible outreach began. The years of painful preparation were over, and the 'real' work of mission could at last begin. The Judsons had determined to go as far as they possibly could to adjust to Burmese cultural expectations, and had studied the way in which Buddhist *zayats* functioned. These were shelters built along main highways where travellers could stop and rest; they were also places of religious refreshment. Buddhist lay teachers would instruct the passers by, and on special occasions Buddhist priests would preach. Adoniram and Ann went to hear one popular preacher and the *Memoir* records the scene:

When all things were properly adjusted, the preacher closed his eyes, and commenced the exercise, which consisted in repeating a portion from their sacred writings. His subject was the conversion of the two prime disciples of Gaudama, and their subsequent promotion and glory. His oratory I found to be entirely different from all that we call oratory. At first, he seems dull and monotonous; but presently, his soft mellifluent tones win their way to the heart, and lull the soul into that state of calmness and serenity, which, to a Burman mind, somewhat resembles the

boasted perfection of their saints of old. His discourse continued about half an hour; and at the close, the whole assembly burst into a short prayer, after which all rose and retired (178).

Adoniram had bought a piece of land behind the mission garden, which lay alongside 'Pagoda Road', the main road joining the city of Rangoon with the great Shwe Dagon Pagoda. Each Burmese Sabbath great crowds thronged this road on their way to worship. He and Ann then supervised the building of the *zayat*. Ann described it as follows:

> The zayat is situated thirty or forty rods from the mission house; and in dimensions, is twenty-seven by eighteen feet. It is raised four feet from the ground, and is divided into three parts. The first division is laid entirely open to the road, without doors, windows, or a partition, in the front side, and takes up a third part of the whole building. It is made of bamboo and thatch, and is the place where Mr. Judson sits all the day long, and says to the passers by, 'Ho! every one that thirsteth,' etc. The next, and middle division, is a large airy room, with four doors and four windows, opening in opposite directions; made entirely of boards, and is whitewashed, to distinguish it from the other zayats around us.

> In this room, we have public worship in Burman on the Sabbath; and in the middle of which I am now situated at my writing table, while six of the male scholars are at one end, each with his torch and black board, over which he is industriously bending, and emitting the curious sounds of the language. The third, and last division, is only an entry way, which opens into the garden, leading to the mission house.

In this apartment, all the women are seated, with their lights and black boards, much in the same position and employment as the men. The black board, on which all the Burmans learn to read and write, answers the same purpose as our slates (179–80).

The missionaries were excited and optimistic about this new development. Ann described the work as follows:

Relative to the mission, it is gaining ground slowly, but I hope surely. We have a place erected for public worship, where Mr. Judson and myself spend the day in conversing with all who call; he with the men, and I with the women. On the Sabbath we have regular public worship in the Burman language. The building is situated in one of the public roads; which, on account of its being lined on both sides with pagodas, is called Pagoda road.

This last week has been a very interesting one to us, on account of having had several very hopeful inquirers, who really appeared to be a prepared people for the Lord. I have a meeting every Wednesday evening with the females, many of whom appear attentive and inquisitive (182).

Further details were supplied in her *Account*:

April 1819. Since Dr. Judson has commenced public preaching in the zayat, I have begun again to have my female meetings, which were given up in consequence of the scattered state of the Burmans around us, at the time of our government difficulties. I attend with them every Wednesday evening at seven o'clock, as they are more at leisure in the evening than any other time. My last meeting was very animating, and the appearance of the

females (thirteen in number, all young married women) very encouraging. Some of them were inquisitive, and after spending two hours seemed loath to go. One said, she appeared to herself like a blind person, just beginning to see. And another said, she believed in Christ, prayed to him daily, and asked what else was necessary to make her a real disciple of Christ. I told her that she must not only *say* that she believed in Christ, but must believe with all her heart. I told her the manner of life would be changed; but one of the best evidences she could obtain would be when others came to quarrel with her and use abusive language, if, so far from retaliating, she felt a disposition to bear with, to pity, and to pray for them. The Burman women are particularly given to quarrelling, and to refrain from it would be a most decided evidence of a change of heart.[1]

By this time (April 1819) Ann was not only undertaking translation work in the Burman language, but also in the Siamese (Thai) language:

I have been attending to the Siamese language for a year and a half. It is a language easy of acquisition, when one has a teacher he understands. I have not found it so difficult as the Burman; but it has been owing, probably, to the teacher's being a Burman, as well as Siamese scholar. There are several thousands of Siamese who live in Rangoon, and who speak and write the pure language of Siam. With the assistance of the teacher, I have made a translation of the Burman catechism, tract, and Matthew. I have also nearly completed a translation of one of their celebrated books into English. It is an account of the incarnation of one of their deities, when he existed in the form of a great elephant (182).

On 29 April 1819 Ann wrote a long letter to her sister, taking stock
of their situation:

My dear Sister M.

Being left alone in my room this afternoon, I know not how I
can spend it more pleasantly than in writing to a dear, far distant
sister, whom I never expect to meet again, until we arrive at our
Father's house in heaven. Though it is seven long years since I
left my native land and scenes of my earliest years, they are as
fresh in my recollection as though it were but yesterday; and the
wound then inflicted every now and then opens and bleeds afresh.
I believe very few females who have left their native country,
have had it in their power to make such sacrifices as myself.
When I think of my pleasant home, and dear Bradford friends;
the flattering prospects and sources of enjoyment which I left, I
am often led to wonder how I was ever made willing to forsake
them, and deliberately embrace a life replete with vicissitudes,
as the present. But my dear sister Mary, a little sacrifice for the
cause of Christ is not worth naming; and I feel it a privilege, of
which I am entirely undeserving, to have had it in my power to
sacrifice my all for him who hesitated not to lay down his life
for sinners. I rejoice that I had a pleasant home, dear friends,
and flattering prospects to relinquish, and that once in my life
I had an opportunity of manifesting my little attachment to
the cause of Christ. I know you often wish to know *certainly*,
whether I still approve of the first step I took in the missionary
cause; and whether, if I had the choice again to make, with my
present knowledge and views of the subject, I should make the
same. Well, I frankly acknowledge that I should do just the same,
with this exception; that I should commence such a life, with

much more fear and trembling on account of my unfitness; and should almost hesitate whether one so vile, so poorly qualified, ought to occupy a sphere of so much usefulness. I do, at times, feel almost ready to sink down in despair, when I realize the responsibility of my situation, and witness my short-comings in duty. If I have grown any in grace since I have left America, it has consisted entirely in an increasing knowledge of my unspeakably wicked heart. As to my real religious enjoyment, I think, generally speaking, I have not experienced more than when in America. I do hope, however, vile as I am, to obtain an inheritance in that better world, where Jesus has prepared mansions for his followers, and will introduce them there himself, sprinkled with his blood, and clothed in his righteousness (180–82).

The day after this letter was written proved to be proved historic. On 30 April 1819, Moung Nau,[2] who was to be the first Burmese convert, visited the *zayat* for the first time. He soon demonstrated every sign of a genuine change of mind and heart. Given the climate of opposition to foreign religion, there could be no ulterior motive for his profession. The missionaries were overjoyed. Ann wrote a letter on 3 June in which she described something of what this conversion involved:

Little did I think, when I last wrote, that I should so soon have the joyful intelligence to communicate, that one Burman has embraced the Christian religion, and given good evidence of being a true disciple of the dear Redeemer. This event, this single trophy of victorious grace, has filled our hearts with sensations, hardly to be conceived by Christians in Christian countries. This circumstance has convinced us, that God can and does operate on the minds of the most dark and ignorant; and that he makes his

own truths, his own word, the instrument of operation. It serves, also, to encourage us to hope, that the Lord has other chosen ones in this place. As Mr. Judson has given some account of the first impressions of this man, and as I have had him particularly under my instruction since his conversion, I will give you some of his remarks in his own words, with which you will be much interested. 'In our religion there is no way to escape the punishment due to sin; but, according to the religion of Christ, he himself has died in order to deliver his disciples. I wish all the Burmans would become his disciples; then we should meet together as you do in your country; then we should all be happy together in heaven. How great are my thanks to Jesus Christ for sending teachers to this country! and how great are my thanks to the teachers for coming! Had they never come and built that zayat, I should never have heard of Christ and the true God. I mourn that so much of my life passed away before I heard of this religion. How much I have lost!' It is peculiarly interesting to see with what eagerness he drinks in the truths from the Scriptures. A few days ago I was reading with him Christ's sermon on the mount. He was deeply impressed, and unusually solemn. 'These words,' said he, 'take hold on my very heart; they make me tremble. Here God commands us to do every thing that is good in secret, not to be seen of men. How unlike our religion is this! When Burmans make offerings to the pagodas, they make a great noise with drums and musical instruments, that others may see how good they are. But this religion makes the mind fear God; it makes it of its own accord fear sin (188–9).

Moung Nau was baptized on 27 June 1819. Adoniram wrote on 4 July:

We have had the pleasure of sitting down, for the first time, at the Lord's table, with a converted Burman; and it was my privilege,—a privilege to which I have been looking forward with desire for many years,—to administer the Lord's supper in two languages (188).

It seemed that at last the longed-for breakthrough had come.

12

'A little, feeble, solitary band': the first Burmese church (1820)

The year 1819 was a year of drama. The opening of the *zayat* and the subsequent conversion of Moung Nau took place against the background of the grim scene at the mission house of the rapid decline of Wheelock and the increasing hostility of his wife. Then a number of sincere enquirers led to the hope of more conversions, but this took place against the backdrop of escalating tension in the city. The missionaries sensed that something was going on but, as is usual under arbitrary dictatorships, the fear was all the more terrible for being unspoken.

At last in June it was heard that the king had 'gone up to amuse himself in the celestial regions'. His successor, Bagyidaw, had taken over in a bloody coup. He was an ardent Buddhist. New pagodas were built, and he was a strong supporter of the Buddhist priesthood. The prospects looked bleak for the mission.

In Rangoon the missionaries found themselves the target of petty harassment, and extortionate demands for money came under a variety of pretexts. As attendance at the *zayat* grew, so did official suspicion. A well-educated teacher named Moung Shwa-gnong had shown considerable interest in the Christian faith. The viceroy of Rangoon made it known that enquiries would be made. The agenda was plain. There was the real prospect of torture and death for those who openly allied with the foreign religion. Attendance at the *zayat* plummeted and by November 1819 the Judsons had temporarily withdrawn to the mission house.

But in the meantime there had been two more genuine conversions, all the more convincing in this situation of growing opposition. Moung Thah-lah and Moung Byaa applied for baptism in November. Adoniram wrote:

Nov. 6. The two candidates for baptism again presented their urgent petition, that they might be baptized; not absolutely in private, but about sunset, away from public observation. We spent some hours in again discussing the subject with them, and with one another. We felt satisfied, that they were humble disciples of Jesus, and were desirous of receiving this ordinance, purely out of regard to his command, and their own spiritual welfare; we felt, that we were all equally exposed to danger, and needed a spirit of mutual candour, and forbearance, and sympathy; we were convinced, that they were influenced rather by desires of avoiding unnecessary exposure, than by that sinful fear, which would plunge them into apostasy, in the hour of trial; and when they assured us, that if actually brought before government, they could not think of denying their Saviour, we could not

conscientiously refuse their request, and therefore agreed to have them baptized to-morrow at sunset.

[*Nov.*] 7. *Lord's day.* We had worship as usual, and the people dispersed. About half an hour before sunset the two candidates came to the zayat, accompanied by three or four of their friends; and, after a short prayer, we proceeded to the spot where Moung Nau was formerly baptized. The sun was not allowed to look upon the humble timid profession. No wondering crowd crowned the overshadowing hill. No hymn of praise expressed the exulting feeling of joyous hearts. Stillness and solemnity pervaded the scene. We felt, on the banks of the water, as a little, feeble, solitary band. But perhaps some hovering angels took note of the event, with more interest than they witnessed the late coronation; perhaps Jesus looked down on us, pitied and forgave our weaknesses, and marked us for his own: perhaps, if we deny him not, he will acknowledge us another day, more publicly than we venture at present to acknowledge him.

In the evening, we all united in commemorating the dying love of our Redeemer; and I trust we enjoyed a little of his gracious presence in the midst of us.

[*Nov.*] 9. This evening is to be marked as the date of the first Burman prayer meeting that was ever held. None present but myself and the three converts. Two of them made a little beginning—such as must be expected from the first essay of converted heathens. We agreed to meet for this purpose every Tuesday and Friday evening, immediately after family worship; which, in the evening, has for some time been conducted in

Burman and English; and which these people, and occasionally
some others, have attended.

[*Nov.*] *14. Lord's Day.* Have been much gratified to find, that
this evening, the *three converts repaired to the zayat, and held a
prayer meeting of their own accord* (195–6).

Notwithstanding this encouragement, Adoniram realized that their
situation was becoming untenable. He wrote on 26 November 1819:

[*Nov.*] *26.* Ever since the affair of Moung Shwa-gnong, there
has been an entire falling off at the zayat. I sometimes sit there
whole days, without a single visitor, though it is the finest part
of the year, and many are constantly passing.

We and our object are now well known throughout Rangoon.
None wish to call, as formerly, out of curiosity; and none dare to
call from a principle of religious inquiry. And were not the leaders
in ecclesiastical affairs confident that we shall never succeed in
making converts, I have no doubt we should meet with direct
persecution and banishment.

Our business must be fairly laid before the emperor. If he
frown upon us, all missionary attempts within his dominions
will be out of the question. If he favour us, none of our enemies,
during the continuance of his favour, can touch a hair of our
heads. But there is a greater than the emperor, before whose
throne we desire daily and constantly to lay the business. O,
Lord Jesus, look upon us in our low estate, and guide us in our
dangerous course! (196–7).

On 22 December 1819 Adoniram Judson, James Colman and Moung Nau left Rangoon for Ava, at that time the capital of Burma. Ann wrote to a friend:

> Soon after the baptism of the two last disciples Mr. J. and Mr. Colman came to a determination to prepare for Ava, and lay their missionary plans before the king and solicit tolerations for the Christian religion. After a fortnight's tedious preparation, in procuring a boat, hiring people, obtaining government orders etc., and after depositing the female part of the missions in the upper story of a huge brick building (which we—Mrs. C. and myself—term a castle), with the Bible in their hands for a present to his majesty, they departed from Rangoon on the 21st of this month and are now on their way to the 'golden feet'. We feel this is a most important era in the Mission. If the king grants permission for the preaching of the gospel, the zayat will again be opened, and other means for its promulgation will be used. But if not, no Burman will venture to examine the religion of Christ and with aching hearts we shall be obliged to leave this idolatrous people, after having seen the power of God displayed in the conversion of four immortal souls. We earnestly wish our Christian friends in Scotland and America were *now* acquainted with the peculiar state of this Mission, that their united prayers might be engaged to prevent the expulsion of the gospel from this country, through the instrumentality of one man. But before they can be made acquainted with it, the important crisis will be passed, we shall either have a wider door opened for usefulness than ever, or we shall be beyond the reach of despotic power.[1]

Judson, Colman and Moung-Nau took a month to travel the 350 miles to Ava. Their mission was perilous in the extreme. Judson and

Colman knew that before their arrival in Burma a national who had converted to Catholicism had been beaten nearly to death. What they did not know was that the man who had informed upon the convert and supervised the torture was now one of the new king's highest-ranking officials. Their request was doomed.

However, they did have one positive contact at the court (then located at Amarapoora, about six miles from Ava). When Adoniram and Ann had arrived in Rangoon, Ann had quickly made friends with the wife of the viceroy Mya-day-men. He had since then been moved to the capital as a public minister of state. Judson and Colman visited him and his wife, presenting costly gifts, and saying that they requested 'leave to behold the Golden Face'. Mya-day-men was able to secure them this privilege, and thus the missionaries were permitted to enter the breathtaking golden splendour of the palace on 27 January 1820. But having listened to the petition, the king just threw a tract presented to him to the ground. Judson's 'last resort' had failed. No subject of Burma was to be allowed to convert to the foreign religion.

On their arrival back in Rangoon on 18 February 1820, Judson and Colman were brutally honest with the Burmese converts. The mission at Rangoon had no chance of success. They proposed to move to Chittagong (see map on page 74), which was situated between Arakan and Bengal and was under British rule. It was also inhabited by Burmese-speaking people. But the three converts pleaded with them to reconsider. They argued that the missionaries could not possibly abandon the good number of serious enquirers. At the very least, they argued, could not the mission be maintained until there was a national church of ten members, a local leader appointed and the work left to propagate itself? Judson and Colman were overwhelmed at the determination and courage of these young believers. The prospect of

opposition had only stiffened their resolve. At last it was decided that Colman and his wife would move to Chittagong to start a mission. This could be a refuge if the position in Rangoon became untenable.[2] In the meantime Adoniram and Ann would remain in Rangoon to build up the tiny church. In March 1820 they found themselves once more alone in the mission house. They felt the urgency of the task as their situation was so fragile. Adoniram wrote:

> O, for toleration—a little toleration. We will be content to baptize in the night, and hold worship in private; but we do pray that we may not be utterly banished from the land; that we may not be cut up root and branch. O, that these poor souls, who are groping in the dark, feeling after the truth, may have time and opportunities to find the precious treasure ... (216).

The following three months saw intense activity. Quite a number of Burmese people were seriously interested in the new faith. Long days were spent in detailed arguments with the enquirers. Many of these were disillusioned with Buddhism. They embraced a system which Judson described as 'semi-atheistic'. He believed that this teaching, regarded by true Buddhists as heretical, was becoming popular in various parts of the country and preparing the way for Christianity. The teacher Moung-Shwa-gnong had in fact taught this 'heresy' in Rangoon for several years. Adoniram wrote:

> Since he has become acquainted with us, he frequently tells his adherents, I know nothing; if you want true wisdom, go to the foreign teacher, and there you will find it (216).

Ann was spending many hours with female enquirers. For example, Adoniram wrote on 20 April 1820:

Mah Men-la and her friends have been with Mrs. Judson all day. She gives increasing evidence of being a true disciple; but is extremely timid, through fear of persecution (214).

Despite continuing work, these were months of painful illness for Ann. Her recurring liver complaint was treated with courses of 'salivation' (see pages 155f.) which produced no relief, only total exhaustion. Reluctantly Adoniram decided that they would have to seek medical help in Calcutta, and thus on 19 July 1820 they sailed for Bengal. 'They were accompanied to the vessel by the native converts, and by a hundred other individuals, who testified sincere grief at their departure' (218).

By this time a total of ten converts had been baptized, including the highly educated teacher, Moung Shwa-gnong, and one woman, Mah Men-la. Adoniram and Ann hated to leave the infant church so soon. But the 'little feeble solitary band' no longer looked so weak. These ten converts had been baptized, knowing full well that in so doing they risked their lives.

13

The prospect of separation (1821)

The voyage from Rangoon to Calcutta took a month (19 July–18 August 1820) and Ann's health had not improved on the way. The Judsons then moved up to Serampore, as the climate there was believed to be as healthy as anywhere in Asia. By November Ann felt sufficiently recovered for plans to be made for their return to Rangoon. They sailed from Calcutta on 23 November, arriving back in Rangoon on 5 January 1821.

How different the prospects were now from when they had first arrived seven and a half years earlier, in July 1813!

Then, all had been unknown. They had been novices, not even knowing, since their change of view on baptism, whether they had any support from home. Now they knew that their application for support had effectively launched the American Baptist missionary movement. The American Baptist Board of Foreign Missions had been formed for their support, and already other missionaries had been sent out.

Then Burma had been the terrifying unknown; the people, language and culture all totally alien. Now Adoniram and Ann had mastered the Burmese language; they had printed tracts and a catechism which had been widely disseminated; Adoniram was well advanced in his translation of the New Testament into Burmese and he had started work on a dictionary. In addition, Ann had learned the Siamese language and had translated the catechism, a basic tract and the Gospel of Matthew into Siamese.

Then, despite Felix Carey's pioneering efforts, there had been no Burmese converts and there was no Burmese church. And now, best of all, they were welcomed back by the members of the first Burmese church, all of whom had persevered during their absence.

Adoniram wrote:

January 5. As we drew near the town, we strained our eyes to distinguish the countenances of our friends amid the crowd that we saw assembled on the wharf. The first that we recognized was the teacher, Moung Shwa-gnong, with his hands raised to his head, as he discerned us on the deck; and, on landing, we met successively with Mah Men-la, and Moung Thah-lah, and several others, men, women, and children, who, after our usual examination at the custom-house, accompanied us to the mission-house. Soon after, Moung Nau and others came in, who had not, at first, heard of our arrival. In the evening, I took my usual seat among the disciples; and when we bowed down in prayer, the hearts of us all flowed forth in gratitude and praise.

[January] 13. Have spent the past week in getting our things in order, and receiving visits from the disciples and inquirers.

Yesterday, Moung Gway, the only one of the baptized whom we had not seen, returned from the woods, on hearing of our arrival; and I am now able to record, (and I do it with the most heart-felt satisfaction and grateful praise to the preserving Saviour,) that though they have, for the space of six months, been almost destitute of the means of grace, and those who lived in our yard have been dispersed, and forced, through fear of heavy extortion and oppression from petty officers of government, to flee into the woods, or take refuge under some government person who could protect them; yet not one of them has dishonoured his profession, but all remain firm in their faith and attachment to the cause (219–20).

January 20. This afternoon Mrs. Judson went to the village of the Nan-dau-gong people, to fix on a spot for the erection of a small school-house. Mah Men-la has, of her own accord, proposed to open a school in the precincts of her house, to teach the girls and boys of the village to read; in consequence of which the latter will not be under the necessity of going to the Burman priests for education, as usual. When we found out that she had really made a beginning, we told her that some of the Christian females in America would, doubtless, defray the expenses of the undertaking ...[1]

[*January*] *21. Lord's day.* All the disciples but one, and all the hopeful inquirers, were present at worship: who, together with some others, made up an assembly of about twenty-five adults, all paying respectful and devout attention; the most interesting assembly, all things considered, that I have yet seen. How impossible it seemed, two years ago, that such a precious

assembly could ever be raised up out of the Egyptian darkness, the atheistic superstition, of this heathen land (220–21).

In 1816 there had been no certainty that their arrival would be tolerated, but now although national prospects for mission were still bleak, at least they had a measure of local acceptance:

> [*January*] 6. In the morning, we went to the government-house. The lady of the viceroy received Mrs. J. with the familiarity of a friend. We sat some time conversing with her. She informed us that she was now Woon-gyee-gah-dau, and was allowed to ride in a wau, (a vehicle carried by forty or fifty men); dignities which very few Burman ladies attain. While we were sitting with her, the viceroy just made his appearance, stalking along, as usual, with his great spear. He looked down upon us a moment, saying, 'Ah! you are come;' and then passed on (219).

Adoniram soon learned that the change of administration in Rangoon had effectively saved the infant church from destruction. The Buddhist teacher Moung Shwa-gnong had been threatened under the previous viceroy. While the Judsons were away, there was another effort to intimidate him:

> Soon after Mya-day-men assumed the government of this province, all the priests and officers of the village, where Moung Shwa-gnong lives, entered into a conspiracy to destroy him. They held daily consultations, and assumed a tone of triumph: while poor Moung Shwa-gnong's courage began to flag—and, though he does not like to own it, he thought he must flee for his life. At length one of the conspiracy, a member of the supreme court, went into the presence of the viceroy, and, in order to sound his

disposition, complained that the teacher, Moung Shwa-gnong, was making every endeavour to turn the priests' rice pot bottom upwards. *What consequence?* said the viceroy, *Let the priests turn it again.* This sentence was enough; the hopes of the conspiracy were blasted; and all the disciples felt they were sure of toleration under Mya-day-men. But this administration will not probably continue many months (220).

With the limited measure of toleration available, the work went forward. The outlook was hopeful. There were so many enquirers to spend time with. There was continuing translation work to be done. Ann was at the very peak of usefulness; having spent nearly eight years mastering two languages, she was more than competent in both translation work and in teaching and counselling enquirers and new converts. But once again ill-health knocked her out of action, and it was increasingly clear that unless she moved right away from the vicious climate of Burma she would soon die. In August Adoniram wrote:

August 4. Am just recovering from the second fit of sickness which I have had this season. The first was the cholera morbus; the present has been a fever. The second day after I was taken, Mrs. J. was taken with the same; and, for several days, we were unable to help one another. Through divine mercy, however, we contrived to get our medicines from time to time, and are now in a convalescent state, so far as the fever is concerned. Mrs. J., however, is suffering severely under the liver complaint, which, notwithstanding continual salivations, is making such rapid and alarming advances, as to preclude all hope of her recovery in this part of the world (222).

Ann and Adoniram then faced an agonizing choice. There was no question but that Ann had to return to America at least temporarily for treatment. She would probably need to be away from Burma for at least two years. Her absence would be a grievous loss to the mission. But if Adoniram were to accompany her the work could well fold up altogether, and the fruit of eight years of labour be threatened. The prospect of separation was terrible, not least with the appalling slowness of communication between Burma and America; a two-year gap was not unknown. But together they came to what they knew was the right decision. Ann would travel alone. Adoniram would stay and continue with the vital translation work and nurture the young church. Ann wrote:

> Those only who have been through a variety of toil and privation, to obtain a darling object, can realize how entirely every fibre of the heart adheres to that object, when secured. Had we encountered no difficulties, and suffered no privations in our attempt to form a church of Christ, under the government of a heathen despot, we should have been warmly attached to the individuals composing it, but should not have felt that tender solicitude and anxious affection, as in the present case.

> Rangoon, from having been the theatre, in which so much of the faithfulness, power, and mercy of God had been exhibited— from having been considered, for ten years past, as my home for life—and from a thousand interesting associations of ideas, had become the dearest spot on earth. Hence you will readily imagine, that no ordinary consideration could have induced my departure (223).

On 21August 1821 Ann left with Emily for Calcutta, arriving on 22 September. As she left, Adoniram wrote a letter to go with her to Hough, now with his family at Serampore. His bleak despair at the thought of losing Ann for so long was lightened only by a sort of desperate humour:

My dear Brother Hough,

I send you herewith Mrs. Judson and all that remains of the blue-pill and senna,[2] and beg you will see the articles all well packed and shipped for America by the earliest safe opportunity. Whatever expenses may be incurred be so good as to defray from your own funds, and transmit your bill to me.

It is said that man is prone to jest in the depth of misery; and the bon-mots of the scaffold have been collected: you may add the above specimen to the list if you like. I feel as if I was on the scaffold, and signing, as it were, my own death-warrant. However, two years will pass away at last. Time and tide wait for no man, heedless alike of our joys and sorrows.

When I last wrote I was in the latter part of Acts; since that time I have done nothing at all. For ten days or a fortnight we were laid by with fever, unable to help one another, and no living soul to depend on but Emily; and since we became convalescent, I have been occupied in making up my mind to have my right arm amputated, and my right eye extracted, which the doctors say are necessary in order to prevent a decay and mortification of the whole body conjugal.[3]

To lose Ann was indeed like losing part of himself, but as the temporary separation seemed to be her only chance of long-term recovery, Adoniram had no choice but to say goodbye, not knowing when—or whether—he would see her again.

14

'This garden of the Lord' (1822)

To leave Adoniram had been heartbreaking. From Calcutta Ann wrote:

> …nothing but the prospect of a final separation would have induced us to decide on this measure … But duty to God, to ourselves, to the Board of Missions, and to the perishing Burmans, compelled us to adopt this course of procedure, though agonizing *to all the natural feelings* of our hearts … (223–4).

Her health had not improved during the sea voyage to Calcutta, and the doctors there insisted that the only cure was departure to a cold climate. To Ann's great disappointment the only possible passage to America was far too expensive. She was forced to accept a place on a ship bound for England which sailed on 5 January 1822. Because she agreed to share a cabin with three children the expenses were all covered by their father. She resolved that if the liver complaint cleared

up during the voyage she would return to Rangoon by return passage
on the same ship, and if not she would try to proceed to America.

On arrival in England it was clear that immediate return to Rangoon
was out of the question. But it was also evident that the work of the
Judsons was much admired, and she was welcomed wherever she went.
All possible measures were taken to make her stay as comfortable and
enjoyable as possible. A Methodist Member of Parliament, Joseph
Butterworth, became her mentor and sponsor. She wrote from his
home in London on 7 June 1822 to a friend in Scotland:

My dear Mrs. Deakin,

From this highly favoured part of the world, this garden of the
Lord, I am allowed the happiness of addressing you. Striking
indeed is the contrast between this splendid city and that wild
idolatrous country where all my former letters to you have been
dated. Yet I cannot say that the same happy sensations pervade
my mind as on former occasions when writing, for though I am
in the Christian world and surrounded by kind dear friends, yet I
am far away from my world, and feel in state of constant anxiety
relative to my little world which is left far behind.[1]

Expenses were provided for an extended stay in the spa town of
Cheltenham, and the Deakins were also offering an all-expenses-paid
trip to Scotland. From Cheltenham Ann wrote again to Mrs Deakin
on 21 June 1822:

My dear Mrs. Deakin,

I have delayed answering your kind letter for several days for the purpose of bringing my mind to a decision relative to visiting Scotland. And after weighing the subject maturely, I am compelled to say that *I ought not to visit* Glasgow. Inclination prompts my setting off immediately, but judgment and reason dissent. Since restoration to health, is my great object, since I have left my dear home in Burmah and subjected myself to a state of continued mental discipline for no other cause, I am convinced that duty demands my rendering subservient to the promotion of my health, every inferior consideration. During my residence in London, my health very sensibly declined, from no other cause than being continually surrounded by dear Christians, whose society was so congenial and interesting to my feelings as to carry them beyond the bounds of their companion, the body and induced that languor and exhaustion from which I have hardly yet recovered. Meeting with my dear Christian friends in Scotland, I am well aware would produce the same effects. I could not be with you my dear Mrs. Deakin without having all my feelings excited or without telling you of the wonderful dealings of our covenant God with us in Burmah, a recital of which quite un-nerves me. This, together with the fatigue necessarily occasioned by the journey and the shortness of my stay in this country, is my reason for my coming to the conclusion that *I ought not to visit Scotland*.

I do most sincerely thank you and dear Mr. Deakin for your urgent request to reside for a few days in your family and I know of nothing that could afford me greater pleasure (excepting an immediate return to Rangoon) than to comply with it. But though we be deprived of the pleasure of an interview on earth, I trust we

shall meet and recognise each other in heaven, where I hope to introduce you to some of the Burman females, as trophies of the wars of Christ, and whose souls are made white by his precious blood. A few more years, and perhaps days, and our work will be done, our toils ended. Let us be faithful unto death and we shall assuredly receive the crown which shall forever distinguish us as the followers of the Lamb.

I have been ordered to Cheltenham to drink the mineral waters. I shall continue ten days longer, when I hope the physician will think me in a safe state to visit America. Please to direct, as before, under cover to Mr. Butterworth, who will know where to find me. I have not heard from Mr. Judson since my arrival in England. Expect to hear every day. Pray for me my dear Mrs. Deakin and believe me.

Very affectionately yours,

Ann Judson.[2]

She changed her mind regarding the trip to Scotland. But her friend Joseph Butterworth felt compelled to try to limit the demands that would be placed on her there. He wrote two urgent letters to her host Mr Deakin, warning of the danger of letting her do too much:

Bedford Square, 20th July, 1822.

Dear Sir,

Mrs. Judson has, of course, informed you that she sets off for Scotland by the steam packet, *James Watts*, early on Wednesday

morning next, and will probably reach Edinburgh on Thursday night or early on Friday.

Perhaps you will write to some person at Edinburgh to meet our very dear friend and conduct her to Glasgow. One should like her to see Mr. Gordon, Mr. Gray, and a very few friends at Edinburgh, but repose is absolutely necessary for her, and if she could be taken away from all society for a short time it would be a great comfort. The excitement of friends is too much for her shattered state. I therefore write this as a charge to you and Mrs. Deakin, that if you wish to preserve the valuable life of our friend you must keep her quiet—her natural vivacity and love of ... [two lines cut away] ... placed under strong coercion. You will, sir, I am sure, pardon this intrusion from a stranger, but I feel too much interest in behalf of our dear friend not to feel it my duty to lay an embargo on her friends that she may not be absolutely destroyed by kindness.

[Signature cut away. It was: Jos. Butterworth.]

Bedford Square, 29th July, 1822.

Dear Sir,

I am truly rejoiced to hear that our dear Mrs. Judson is safely arrived in Scotland, but finding that she is in very great danger of being absolutely killed by kindness, I take the liberty of writing once more to caution my good friends, Mr. and Mrs. Deakin of *their danger*. They are altogether responsible for the life and health of our friend so far as human means only are concerned.

I am induced to write in this cautionary strain as I find Mrs.
J. was quite well on board the steam packet, *when she was quiet*,
but since she arrived in Edinburgh her pain has returned, and I
know this to be occasioned by company and excitement. Repose
is absolutely necessary for her delicate frame—her recovery is
doubtful and the best means should be devised for her restoration.

Mrs. J.'s own words to me are—'Here [at Edinburgh] I am
surrounded by these warm-hearted Scotch people, who are *ready
to eat me up.*'

Now, my dear sir, the agitation which Mrs. J. must naturally
feel at the prospect of being 'eaten alive' cannot mend her health,
and I must request that both you and Mrs. Deakin will allay her
fears and place her in some situation of *safety*.

I have just received the enclosed lamentation from the young
man I employed to land our good friend at Edinburgh, which
you will be pleased to hand over to Mrs. Judson. I trust that the
interviews which Mrs. J. will have with friends in Scotland will
be rendered mutually profitable.

With kindest regards to Mrs. Judson and Mrs. Deakin,

I am, Dear Sir, Your faithful

Jos. Butterworth.[3]

While Ann was in Scotland, the American Baptist Board sent a
request that she return to America, saying they would provide the
fare for the trip in the New York packet. A number of women in

Liverpool intervened and raised the funds for her to travel in a much more comfortable ship. She sailed for America on 16 August 1822, just about a year after having left Rangoon. She wrote:

> *August 16.* Embarked on board the *Amity*, for the United States. Mr. and Mrs. Deakin, Miss Hope, Miss Jones and her brother, accompanied me about fifty miles, and returned in the steamboat. After the departure of these dear friends, I felt sad and disconsolate, being quite alone, without any Christian friend on board, or any female with whom I can converse. Yet I am not alone. The same kind and glorious Being, who, notwithstanding all my provocations, has hitherto directed my steps, and at times granted me his presence, is still, I trust, with me, and will make my way prosperous. I hope to enjoy much of his presence, during my passage, and spend more time, in the immediate duties of religion, than my late rambling life has admitted. Should I be preserved through the voyage, the next land I tread will be my own native soil, ever loved America, the land of my birth. I cannot realize that I shall ever again find myself, in my own dear home at Bradford, amid the scenes of my early youth, where every spot is associated with some tender recollection. But the constant idea, that my dear J. is not a participator of my joys, will mar them all (227–8).

15

Return to America (1822–1823)

Ann returned to America ten and a half years after that 'trying scene of parting' in February 1812. Then the four new missionaries had been so young and idealistic; Adoniram at twenty-three, Samuel Newell just a little older, Ann twenty-two, Harriet nineteen. Now both Harriet and Samuel were dead, but Ann and Adoniram had proved themselves, a mission in Burma had been established and others had followed. Ann had never expected to see her mother, father and sisters again. The anticipation itself threw her into a nervous state, and all the excitement of this return trip very nearly defeated its object. The ship arrived in New York on 25 September 1822 and Ann took a steamboat to Philadelphia. From there she wrote to her parents-in-law on 27 September:

> My dear Parents,
>
> With mingled sensations of joy and sorrow, I address a few lines to the parents of my beloved husband—joy, that I once more find

myself in my own native country, and with the prospect of meeting
with loved relatives and friends—sorrow, that he who has been a
participator in all my concerns for the last ten years, is not now
at hand to partake with me in the joyful anticipations of meeting
those he so much loves. I left Liverpool on the 16th of August, and
arrived in New-York harbour day before yesterday. On account of
the prevalence of the yellow fever, prudence forbade my landing.
Accordingly I embarked on board the steam-boat for this place,
where I arrived a few hours ago. It was my intention to pass a
week in Philadelphia, and then go to Providence, and thence to
you in Woburn, as it would be on my way to Bradford, where I
shall spend the winter. But Dr. Staughton wishes me to go to
Washington, which will detain me in this part of the country a
week longer. However, I hope to be with you in a fortnight from
this time. My health is much improved since I left England, and
I begin to hope that the disorder is entirely eradicated (229–30).

Ann found herself drawn into a whirlwind of activity. All her
family and friends wanted to see her. Her arrival had been eagerly
anticipated by numerous Baptists who wished to see one of their very
first missionaries in person. Far from leading to recovery, it seemed
that her arrival back in her homeland was likely to result in a complete
breakdown, both physical and nervous. Her brother-in-law, Elnathan
Judson, intervened. He was a doctor and insisted that the rigours of
a winter in New England would be too much for her. She should, he
advised, travel south to Baltimore, where he lived. If she spent the
winter there he could oversee her medical treatment. Reluctantly Ann
agreed. All her natural inclinations were to spend as much time as
possible with her family. After all, this might well be the last time they
would ever be together. But the whole purpose of this trip, and the only
justification for her separation from Adoniram and the mission, was

the recovery of her health. If continued time with family and friends was going to damage it, she would have to leave them.

Ann described the decision to move south in a letter from Baltimore, dated 19 December 1822, to her friend Mrs Chaplin:

> Relative to my leaving New-England for the south, when you shall hear my reasons, you will, I dare say, join with me in thinking, that duty to myself and Mr. Judson required my proceeding as I have. I had never *fully* counted the cost of a visit to my dear native country and beloved relatives. I did not expect that a scene which I had anticipated *as so joyous*, was destined to give my health and constitution, a shock which would require months to repair. During my passage over from England, my health was most perfect, not the least symptom of my original disorder remained. But from the day of my arrival, the idea that I was once more on American ground, banished all peace and quiet from my mind, and for the first four days and nights, I never closed my eyes to sleep! This circumstance, together with my dwelling on my anticipated meeting with my friends, occasioned the most alarming apprehensions. Still, however, I flattered myself, that after my first meeting with my friends was over, I should gradually recover my composure, and hastened my departure for the eastward. I reached my father's in about a fortnight after my arrival in this country—and had not been able to procure a single night's sleep: the scene which issued brought my feelings to a crisis, nature was quite exhausted, and I began to fear would sink. To be concise, my dear Mrs. Chaplin, my health began to decline in the most alarming manner, and the pain in my side and cough returned. I was kept in a state of constant excitement, by daily meeting with my old friends and

acquaintances; and during the whole six weeks of my residence at my father's, I had *not one* quiet night's rest. I felt the cold most severely, and found, as that increased, my cough increased.

You may not perhaps be aware of the circumstance, that Mr. Judson's only brother is a physician of some considerable skill, under government, and located for the winter in this city. During my stay at Bradford, his letters were most frequent and urgent, relative to my removal to the south, for the purpose of salivating, as the most dangerous consequences would ensue, should I, with my Indian constitution, salivate at the north. I saw that my disorder was rapidly gaining ground—my nervous system had become so much affected, that the very sight of an old dear friend was quite distressing, and I really desired to get away from the sight of every human being, as it had become very painful to talk. Thus situated, there was no hope of my recovery, as my father's house was thronged with visitors from day to day. Painful as it was to think of leaving my beloved family, I felt convinced, since it was my only object in visiting this country, duty required that every thing should yield to endeavours to regain my health. I knew that retirement, freedom from company and excitement, were as necessary as a milder climate, neither of which could be obtained at Bradford. My sister had made arrangements to accompany me; but meeting in Boston with a pious man going on to Washington, and knowing I should receive the kindest attention when once with my brother, I desired her to return to Bradford, to comfort my parents.

I have been in this city about a fortnight, and am very comfortably situated with my brother at a boarding-house, where I refuse to see company of any description till my health

is re-established. I find the climate mild and delightful—have the best medical attendance in the city, through the influence of my brother—have commenced a course of mercury, which I trust, through the blessing of God, will perfectly restore my health—and find my nervous system so far restored to its usual state, that I am able to study four or five hours every day. This, to me, is an unspeakable comfort, as I hope my time will not be entirely lost in my endeavours to regain my health (233–5).

The months of quiet in Baltimore were just what Ann needed. The weeks of intense attention from so many people in England, Scotland and then in New England had been flattering but oppressive. She felt spiritually dry, and in need of space and time without a constant stream of visitors. She also sensed the danger of being the object of unremitting attention and praise, as the same letter to Mrs Chaplin indicates:

Your kind hint, relative to my being injured by the lavish attention of our dear friends in this country, has much endeared you to my heart. I am well aware that human applause has a tendency to elate the soul, and render it less anxious about spiritual enjoyments, particularly if the individual is conscious of deserving them. But I must say, my dear Mrs C. that since my return to this country, I have often been affected to tears, in hearing the undeserved praises of my friends, feeling that I was far, very far, from being what they imagined; that there are thousands of poor, obscure Christians, whose excellences will never be known in this world, who are a thousand times more deserving of the tender regard of their fellow Christians than I am. Yet I trust, I am grateful to my heavenly Father for inclining the hearts of his children to look on me with a friendly eye. The

retired life I now lead, is much more congenial to my feelings, and much more favourable to religious enjoyment, than when in England and America, where I was kept in a continual bustle of company. Yes, it is in retirement that our languishing graces are revived, our affections raised to God, and our souls refreshed and quickened by the influences of the Holy Spirit. If we would live near the threshold of heaven, and daily take a glance of our promised inheritance, we must avoid, not only worldly, but religious dissipation. Strange as it may seem, I do believe there is something like religious dissipation, in a Christian's being so entirely engrossed in religious company, as to prevent his spiritual enjoyments (235–6).

Only by withdrawing from the attention of friends and family could Ann devote herself to writing. And her production of *An Account of the American Baptist Mission to the Burman Empire* resulted in a great upsurge of interest in the mission. This publication did far more than she could have done in person to promote the work of the Baptist Missionary Society. She described its progress to Mrs Chaplin:

While in England, my friends repeatedly urged my writing an account of the Burman Mission, as so little information had hitherto been communicated. On my passage over I made a beginning, in a 'Series of Letters addressed to Mr. Butterworth,' in whose house I resided during my stay in England. While at Bradford, I was unable to proceed in this work; but since my arrival here, my freedom from interruption has enabled me to go on—and I find much pleasure in the consideration, that I shall be able to give to my friends, not only in England, but in America, that information relative to the Burman empire, which my state of health forbids my verbally communicating. My

object is, to give an account of the American Baptist Mission to Burmah—its origin, progress, and success; consisting principally in a compilation of those letters and documents transmitted to friends in America, interspersed with accounts of the population, manners, and customs of the Burmans (235).

Education for girls in Burma was one of Ann's most cherished schemes. Her *Address to Females in America*, written in Boston in November 1822 (see Appendix II), was designed to raise awareness and funds, and royalties from the *Account* were to be used for the same purpose. The preface to the 1823 London edition of the *Account* explained that slavery was common in the Burmese Empire, and orphans were especially vulnerable:

> To redeem a few female slaves of this description, is an object which Mrs. Judson proposes to herself, on her return to Rangoon in order to commence with them a system of instruction; hoping that, should her labours succeed, their conduct in after life may convince the Burmans of the utility of female education. The profits from this publication, if any should arise, will be appropriated to the redemption from slavery and education, of female children on Mrs. Judson's approaching return to Burmah.[1]

Did these months in the south achieve the purpose of restoring her health? It seems not. Any benefit she felt was due to the mild climate, the peace and quiet and the good diet. It is probable that the medical treatments used for her liver complaint did more harm than good. Medicine at that time followed the ancient belief that the humours (or fluids) in the body had to be balanced out. The methods used were drastic and painful: bleeding with leeches and blistering were popular and, worst of all, 'salivating' with mercury. Benjamin

Rush (1745–1813), a signatory of the Declaration of Independence, was the 'founding father' of American medicine. He believed that 'a hyperactive state of the arteries (he called it hypertension) was the key to disease'.[2] This demanded copious blood-letting, a painful and disgusting business. 'The slug-like leech used to suck blood is one and a half inches long, expanding to six inches on feeding. It has 10 stomachs down each side.'[3] Rush also believed firmly in the efficacy of mercury: he called it a 'safe and nearly a universal medicine'.[4] Thus doctors commonly recommended calomel (mercurous chloride) purges, and the ubiquitous 'blue pills'. It seems staggering that blue pills containing mercury were the standard treatment for all manner of complaints in the early nineteenth century. It was not realized that mercury is lethal in its effects on the body, attacking the central nervous system.[5] Exposure to mercury can result in exhaustion, weight loss, dizziness, insomnia, headaches, mental confusion and loss of co-ordination. Ann, not surprisingly, found the courses of treatment that winter utterly debilitating. She wrote on Christmas Day 1822, to her sister Mary:

My dear Sister Mary,

Many thanks for the concern you manifest for my spiritual health, as it is to me a convincing evidence that you constantly pray for me. Whatever is my situation, however flattering my prospects of a worldly nature, all is loss and dross unless I feel something of that spiritual peace and comfort which our Lord bequeathed to his disciples. And I know of no means so directly calculated to ensure this peace to us, as the fervent and earnest prayers of those who enter heaven, as it were, to lay the case of their friends before their Father. I am in this city much more comfortably situated than you imagine, or I anticipated. I have

always found full employment of time, and much retirement from company of every description, the grand secret for living near to God, and the right performance of these duties incumbent on us. In these respects I have not been so comfortably situated since I left Rangoon, as now, excepting on my passage from England to this country. When I first arrived, I requested the servants of the house to say, when any person requested to see me, that 'Mrs. Judson did not see company.' For I felt resolved that my health should be my first consideration.

Brother E. is absent, engaged in his official duties, nearly all day, so that I have the disposal of my time entirely. I spend about five hours in the day in arranging letters, relative to the Burman Mission; and feel very happy in the consideration, that in my endeavours to regain my health, my time is not all lost—for in this publication Christians will have a more correct view of the little church in Rangoon, when they see from what materials it has been raised, than I could give them by conversing months. In addition to these advantages, I have an assistant copyist, a pious, excellent young lady. I have been here three weeks, but have not been out of the house, and scarcely out of my chamber, since my arrival. I have the best and most experienced medical attendance in the city. The physicians here say I should not have lived through the winter in New England. They have thought it best to salivate me; and am now under a course of mercury, and feel my mouth considerably affected. My cough has been very severe, until within two days past, and I trust, in consequence of the mercury, it is beginning to subside. The physicians say there is no doubt but I shall recover by spring; but I desire to leave it with Him, who seeth the end from the beginning, and who doeth all things well. Why am I spared? O may it be to promote

the cause of Christ in Burmah, and to be successful in winning
souls. May we make it our great business to grow in grace, and
to enjoy closet religion. Here is the place for us to prepare for
usefulness. I have received several good spiritual letters since I
have been here—one from Scotland (236–8).

In early January she wrote:

It is nearly three weeks, since I commenced my old employment
of taking mercury. I am now in a state of salivation, my cough is
almost entirely removed, the pain in my side has subsided … I
continue, however, to take mercury, and shall probably be kept
in this state for three weeks to come … (238).

Not surprisingly, her health worsened. More painful and ineffectual
treatment was on the way. In February 1822 she wrote:

For the last month, I have been very feeble—hardly able to
write to any one. I have had two slight attacks of bleeding at the
lungs; and in consequence of this, have been reduced very low
by bleeding at the arm. I have been bled five times, and think I
am now getting better … (239).

To another friend she wrote that she had been 'bled so frequently,
and so largely' (240) that she was totally exhausted. By the end of
February she was longing to return to her family in New England, but
she was too weak to travel. She revised her plans and hoped to move
north at the end of March, but warned her sisters that her continued
exhaustion meant that she would not be able to visit or receive company.
Having returned from Rangoon with a liver complaint, she was now

troubled with a lung complaint. There must have been the unspoken question of whether the whole trip had been a mistake.

Throughout this painful and lonely winter, Ann resolutely held fast to the conviction that God was overruling her circumstances. A letter to her sister on 25 February shows that her heart was still firmly with the work in Burma:

My dear Sister,

From the tenor of my last, I know you will all feel anxious to hear from me, consequently I take the earliest opportunity to write you. My health is daily improving; but after being reduced so low as I have been, by bleeding from the arm, I must expect to gain very gradually. My liver complaint seems entirely removed, and were I not so very feeble, would set off for Bradford to-morrow. But I can now ride only an hour at a time, and am much fatigued after that. But God has been kind, unspeakably kind to me, and enabled me to cast all my cares and concerns on him; and I have frequently been led to say, it is good for me to be afflicted. There are some spiritual, heavenly-minded Christians in this place, who have often refreshed me by their conversation and prayers. A few days ago, I had a prayer meeting in my chamber, and I trust Christ was one in the midst of us. Dr. Staughton sent me yesterday, Mr. Judson's journal, lately received. God is doing wonders in Rangoon, and building up his little church there. Five more have been baptized, making eighteen in all, and several others seriously inquiring. Three females have lately been baptized, who formerly attended my Wednesday meeting. They have set up, of their own accord, a *female prayer meeting*. Is not this encouraging? (241).

She found that there was increasing pressure exerted to prevent her return to Burma:

> I find it is the opinion of my London physicians, that I shall *not live* if I return to the east. Friends in England say, Mr Judson must come there. But I say no—I must make another trial ... (238)

Friends in America urged that at least she remain another year in America to try to rebuild her shattered strength. But Ann was determined to return to Rangoon, if possible in the spring of 1823. Her book was finished and printed in March. She managed to visit friends, family and other contacts in Bradford, Plymouth, Saugus, Charlestown, Cambridge and Salem, and then sailed for Calcutta on 22 June.

Ann travelled with two new missionaries, Jonathan and Deborah Wade, and she used the time on the voyage to teach them the rudiments of the Burmese language. They arrived in Calcutta on 19 October. There they were strongly advised not to proceed to Rangoon, as war seemed imminent between Britain and Burma. But having got this far, Ann and the Wades were not to be deterred. They sailed from Calcutta in November and arrived in Rangoon on 5 December 1823. Ann described the journey home in a letter written from Rangoon on 11 December, shortly after her arrival:

> On the 22nd June last, with a joyful heart, I left my native shores for India, followed by the prayers of thousands, who were collected on the wharf to witness our departure. In a fine new ship, a large airy cabin, with a kind obliging captain, I found myself most pleasantly situated, and under the direction of our

heavenly Father, the winds and waves were propitious, for we reached the sand heads in the Bay of Bengal in a hundred and five days from Boston. During our voyage, I had the happiness of witnessing a most decided change in the captain, who, for two months previously to our arrival at Calcutta, devoted his whole time to the subject of religion, and is resolved, on his return passage, to conduct worship himself among his sailors on the Sabbath.

On my arrival in Bengal, you will readily imagine my first inquiries were to ascertain what intelligence had been received from Mr. Judson, and what prospects of my speedy departure. The information received from the former was animating and encouraging; but respecting the latter, sad indeed, as it was expected that no ship would sail for several months, as very serious difficulties existed between the Burman and British Governments. For several days my mind was in a state of constant anxiety, but was instantaneously relieved, by noticing a paragraph in the paper, advertising a ship for Rangoon. I immediately engaged my passage, and after a month's residence in the kind and hospitable family of the Rev. Mr. Thomason, I embarked for Rangoon, where I safely arrived in nineteen days.[6]

What had this long trip to America achieved? The immediate objective, the restoration of Ann's health, seems to have failed. But the months in Baltimore had enabled Ann to complete her *Account of the American Baptist Mission*. This was widely circulated in America and England, and served to raise the awareness of the religious public of the situation in Burma. Moreover, she was able to meet with a committee appointed by the Baptist General Convention and she made a number of suggestions concerning the mission which were implemented. Her

trip had effectively operated as a most successful promotion of the mission. She had endeared herself to many, and the American public was thus the more appalled by her subsequent experiences and early death. Dr Francis Wayland, the President of Brown University and later the official biographer of Adoniram, described his impressions of Ann during this trip:

It was my good fortune to become intimately acquainted with Mrs. Judson during this visit to the United States. I do not remember ever to have met a more remarkable woman. To great clearness of intellect, large powers of comprehension, and intuitive female sagacity, ripened by the constant necessity of independent action, she added that heroic disinterestedness which naturally loses all consciousness of self in the prosecution of a great object. These elements, however, were all held in reserve, and were hidden from public view by a veil of unusual feminine delicacy. To an ordinary observer, she would have appeared simply a self-possessed, well-bred, and very intelligent gentlewoman. A more intimate acquaintance would soon discover her to be a person of profound religious feeling, which was ever manifesting itself in efforts to impress upon others the importance of personal piety. The resources of her nature were never unfolded until some occasion occurred which demanded delicate tact, unflinching courage, and a power of resolute endurance even unto death. When I saw her, her complexion bore that sallow hue which commonly follows residence in the East Indies. Her countenance at first seemed, when in repose, deficient in expression. As she found herself among friends who were interested in the Burman mission, her reserve melted away, her eye kindled, every feature was lighted up with enthusiasm,

and she was everywhere acknowledged to be one of the most fascinating of women.[7]

16

A joyful reunion (1823)

Meanwhile, back in Burma, Adoniram had been missing Ann intensely. He wrote, soon after her departure from Rangoon on 21 August 1821, that at one level he just longed to find 'some quiet resting-place' where they could be together. But, he reflected, 'Life is short. Happiness consists not in outward circumstances. Millions of Burmans are perishing.'[1] They had to place their own happiness in second place to the work of the kingdom of God. Characteristically, Adoniram threw himself into the work of translation.

For the first four months of Ann's absence, he had no European companion at the mission. Then on 4 December 1821 Jonathan Price arrived with his wife and little girl. Price was an ordained minister, but also had training as a doctor. His skill at removing eye cataracts quickly made him something of a celebrity around Rangoon. Tragically, his wife did not survive for long in the tropical climate. She died of fever on 2 May 1822. Jonathan and Adoniram buried her near to the Judsons' baby boy. The Prices' daughter was sent over to Calcutta, where

another missionary family took care of her. By this time Judson and Price had another family for company, as the Houghs had returned from Serampore in January 1822. By the summer of 1822 eight more converts had been baptized, bringing the total to eighteen.

When the king heard of the American doctor's 'miraculous' ability to remove cataracts, he summoned Price to his royal residence at Ava. Jonathan did not have sufficient command of the language to travel alone, so Adoniram accompanied him, leaving the Houghs to lead the mission at Rangoon. Judson and Price arrived at court on 27 September. Very soon the king interrogated Judson on his work. He asked straight out whether there were any Burmese converts to Christianity. Judson could not lie, and admitted that there were. Amazingly, the king let this pass.

During the following weeks and months Price and Judson found that the official attitude towards them was increasingly sympathetic. They became known and even liked by various members of royalty and government. Judson found himself in deep theological and philosophical conversations with some, including one of the princes. Some leading members of court seemed to be genuinely considering belief in an eternal God. They admitted the logical impossibility of atheism. Judson had the opportunity to preach before the king, albeit briefly, and one of the chief ministers, Moung Zah, had the temerity to say to the king, 'Nearly all the world, your majesty, believe in an eternal God, all except Burmah and Siam, these little spots!'[2] If these opportunities and contacts proved to be useful in the future protection of the church in Burma, the benefits gained by time spent in Ava would outweigh the frustration of being away from the mission and translation work.

In between bouts of fever, Adoniram wrestled with the endless layers of Burmese bureaucracy to try to secure a plot of land on which to build a house—potentially a mission at the very heart of the Burman Empire. Land was leased, and a small hut built by the end of January 1823. Adoniram left one of his converts in charge of the property during his return to Rangoon, and left Ava on 25 January 1823. The king himself extended an invitation for him to return once Mrs Judson had come back from America. Thus Judson planned to return with Ann to start a mission in Ava. The opportunity was thrilling, for if a church could be established in the capital, the principle of religious toleration might be established for the whole empire. In the meantime, however, the missionary zeal of Price seems to have been eroded. Perhaps he was intoxicated by the experience of being treated as a celebrity at court.

On 22 October 1822 Adoniram had received his first letter from Ann since her departure a year and two months before. The eight-page letter had been written during the voyage to England, and her main news was the conversion of several of her fellow-travellers. Once Adoniram arrived back in Rangoon on 5 February 1823 he was impatient to organize the move to Ava; the window of opportunity there might be open for such a short time. But the weeks and months dragged by. During the whole of 1823 there was no letter, no word of when she might return. The situation of the young church in Rangoon was discouraging. Some of the members had left the area to escape the demands of the greedy viceroy. Some had been denounced by their families, and their huts destroyed. One had died. Only three or four remained at the mission. Adoniram made use of the time in completion of his translation of the New Testament. He also prepared a summary of the Old Testament in the Burmese language. This consisted of an outline of Scripture history and a summary of all the main prophecies concerning Christ.

Despite burying himself in work, he found that the time dragged by. On 5 December 1823 he finally resigned himself to face the worst. Maybe she would never return! When Ann arrived back later that very same day, he greeted her with a measure of disbelief. Ann described their reunion in a letter to Josiah Butterworth which was included as a supplement to the *Account*:

> I dare not attempt to describe my feelings as the ship advanced towards the Burman coast. It was late in the evening when the vessel anchored; but the first object which caught my eye, as the boat rowed toward the shore, was Mr. Judson. From long expectation and disappointment, he had acquired such an habitual sadness and dejection of spirit, that it required all my exertion to disperse it, and make him Mr. J. again. He had not heard a word from me for thirteen months, (owing to the failure of my letters) and the very day I arrived, he had in despair yielded all hope of my existence! I soon had the happiness of meeting Mah-Men-lay, Moung-Shay-bay, and others who are still an honour to their profession. May-Myat-lay, the second female who was baptized, died in the triumphs of hope a few months ago. She longed for the hour of her release, and assured those who stood around her that she would soon be in the presence of Christ. Is not this one instance of the power of divine grace more than a compensation for all our days of darkness and distress, formerly spent in preparation for our work?[3]

The reunion was joyful, but Adoniram was not prepared to waste any more time. He was determined to return as soon as possible to Ava. So he did not even take Ann's bags and baggage into the mission house: they were transferred straight onto a boat bound for Ava. Ann explained the move in the same letter, assuring Mr Butterworth that

she would be implementing her scheme for female education in Ava as soon as possible:

> Mr. Judson has his boats in readiness to proceed to Ava, and to-morrow we go on board. He has obtained considerable favour from high officers in Government, and thinks our prospects at Ava very encouraging. The King's own brother, a very powerful prince, has his attention excited by the Christian religion, and has lately written a very kind, affectionate letter to Mr. Judson, requesting his speedy return to Ava, and to bring with him all the sacred books. A foreign female has never yet been introduced to the Burman Court, consequently much curiosity is excited by the expectation of my arrival. May the God of Heaven be our protector, and give us that wisdom which is profitable to direct. I feel, my dear friend, that I am about to begin anew my missionary work, and need more grace, more resolution, and more spirituality of feeling than ever before. We shall be surrounded by despotism and idolatry, but the God of Jacob is our hope, and in his hands we are as safe as in our own loved America. He has evidently pointed out to us the path of duty, and shall we fear to follow where he leads? It is easy for God to open the heart of the King and Queen, and make them a nursing father and mother to the little church in Burmah. We cannot hope and expect too much from God. He has commanded us to open our mouths wide, and he will fill them.

> You shall hear from me on my arrival at the capital, for I am resolved to keep you acquainted with all our steps. I write this in great haste, being surrounded by women and children, who are waiting their final instructions. My schools will commence at Ava; my hopes respecting them are very sanguine. I am much gratified

by your remarks relative to 'The History of the Burman Mission.' The first edition was all sold before I left America, though in so poor a dress. Please to transmit to Mr. Lawson (who is the Agent for our Board) all the money that has been collected for the school, with this direction:—'For Mrs. Judson's Schools in the Burman Empire.' I will give a particular and faithful account of the commencement and progress of my darling plan, for the information of those who are interested in the schools. Mr. Judson would write, but every moment of his time is employed in preparing and arranging our baggage. He will write after our arrival at Ava.

The translation of the New Testament is finished. We will send you a copy of the whole when printed.[4]

They left exactly a week after her arrival, sailing on 13 December and arriving in Ava on 23 January 1824. Adoniram and Ann, delighted to be together, had nearly six weeks on the boat in which they could catch up on two years and four months apart. There was so much news to share, and prospects for their mission had never seemed so good. The last letter from Price to Adoniram had said that the king continued to ask when the Judsons would return, and that the queen was anxious to meet Mrs Judson. Ann was in high spirits, and described part of the journey as follows:

On the Arah-wah-tee, Dec. 31, 1823.

Come, my dear friend, transport yourself for a few moments from your retired home, and refresh your imagination with a view of our floating conveyance majestically passing the fertile banks of the Arah-wah-tee [Irrawaddy]. And had your eye the

same power as imagination, could it rove with equal rapidity over this widely extended globe, it would doubtless be induced to rest on worthier and more interesting objects, but could not find two happier than your friend Ann and her beloved Judson. It is one of those bright days peculiar to an Indian clime; the cool refreshing breezes from the mountains with which we are now encircled, while they unite with the influence of the sun to produce a most delightful temperature of air, invigorate our frames and exhilarate our spirits; the verdure and variety of scenery exhibited on the banks of this noble river, every where interspersed with native villages, and peasants' tents, all conspire to increase those pleasant sensations which our peculiar situation and circumstances are calculated to excite. Our boat is so curiously constructed, and so unlike every thing in your civilized part of the world, that I hardly know in what language to give a description so as to present it clearly to your view: it is a rude uncouth thing, and could you behold it floating down the river Thames, you might imagine that some ingenious fisherman had attached a pair of wings to his little hut, and was conveying it on a boat to your great metropolis, to gratify the curious gaze of the idle multitude. It is fifty feet in length and seven in width. Our rooms or cabins, two in number, are built on the top, the boat being too shallow to admit any thing of the kind within, and constructed in the form of a Burman house, with a sloping roof. The rooms extend half the length of the boat, the one we occupy is made of rough boards, with a thatched roof, the other (occupied by the servants) of bamboo and mats. The wings are formed by the extension of the floor on each side, which makes a passage for the boatmen, without entering our rooms. This heavy unwieldy thing is urged forward almost entirely by manual force, and is either drawn with ropes by the boatmen walking on the

banks, or pushed by long poles. But so strong is the current at this season, and the wind always against us, that our progress is slow indeed. Yet in the midst of these inconveniences and privations, we are happy, because the object we have in view will bear examination. Were we thus penetrating into the heart of this heathen empire for the purpose of accumulating property, or gaining honour or renown, from our fellow-creatures, it would not be an object sufficient to support our minds under present circumstances, and in anticipation of future evils. But we are assured that we are in the service of Him who governs the world, who has said to his disciples, 'Go into all the world,' etc.; and this is our support, and the reward of all our exertions, 'Lo, I am with you *always*, even to the end of the world,' Not a hair of our head can be injured, but with the permission of Him whose precious name we would make known to these unenlightened heathen. Yes, my dear friend, the consideration of the object we have in view, and the brightening prospects relative to ultimate success, fill us with joy, and make us happy, though in this rude solitary boat, far, far away from all Christian society, and no individual associate besides ourselves. Our faithful Moung-Ing is the only native Christian with us, the others being at present scattered according to circumstances. Three are already at Ava waiting our arrival, and Meh-men-lay and others will follow, as soon as their domestic concerns will allow. Moung-Ing, with whom you are already well acquainted, is a firm, solid, and consistent Christian. He unites with us daily in family worship, and frequently leads in prayer, in our occasional religious conferences, when he exhibits much spiritual feeling and strength of intellect. We intend him for the teacher of our girls' school, the commencement of which is I trust just at hand …

A few days ago we had an especial cause of gratitude to God for his preserving care, when in imminent danger. In passing through one of the strong rapids, with which this river abounds, the rudder struck the bottom, which turned the boat immediately across the current, and laid her on her side. It being a cold morning our door was shut, and the boat being on her side, it was some moments before we could get it open, which circumstance for a short time occasioned us to feel all the horrors of shipwreck. Every thing outside of the cabins, such as rice, cooking utensils, and the boatmen's mats were all afloat. The steersman, however, had presence of mind enough to cut the rudder from the boat, which enabled the boatmen to raise her from her side, and after drawing her to the shore, and repairing her rudder, we proceeded on our way, feeling more than ever our dependence on God, and the importance of having our minds at all times stayed on him.[5]

A letter home to her family described the river journey:

Our boat was small and inconvenient; but the current at this season is so very strong, and the wind always against us, that our progress was slow indeed. The season however was cool and delightful; we were preserved from dangers by day and robbers by night, and arrived in safety in six weeks. The Arah-wah-tee is a noble river; its banks every where covered with immortal beings, destined to the same eternity as ourselves. We often walked through the villages; and though we never received the least insult, always attracted universal attention. A foreign female was a sight never before beheld, and all were anxious that their friends and relatives should have a view. Crowds followed us through the villages, and some who were less civilized than others, would run some way before us, in order to have a *long*

look as we approached them. In one instance, the boat being some time in doubling a point we had walked over, we seated ourselves down, when the villagers as usual assembled, and Mr. Judson introduced the subject of religion. Several old men who were present, entered into conversation, while the multitude was all attention. The apparent schoolmaster of the village coming up, Mr. Judson handed him a tract, and requested him to read. After proceeding some way, he remarked to the assembly, that such a writing was worthy of being copied, and asked Mr. Judson to remain while he copied it. Mr. Judson informed him he might keep the tract, on condition he read it to all his neighbours. We could not but hope the Spirit of God would bless those few simple truths, to the salvation of some of their souls (270–71).

There was just one drawback. The prospect of war between Great Britain and Burma was looming. Indeed, during Ann's stopover at Calcutta she and the Wades had been strongly advised not to return to Burma. Jonathan Wade had written from Rangoon on their arrival:

> We arrived in Calcutta on the 19th of October … We were informed that there was a great prospect of war between the English and Burmans. On this account, we were urgently advised by all the friends in Serampore and Calcutta not to venture ourselves in Rangoon. This advice was enforced by an account of the real state of things, kindly afforded for the purpose, by the chief secretary of the government of Bengal. Notwithstanding, we felt it our duty, if an opportunity offered, to venture, trusting in the great Arbiter of life and death for protection … The prospect of war has been daily increasing ever since we arrived. We cannot predict the final issue, but we pray that it may be for the advancement of the object of this Mission (268–9).

The chief secretary in Bengal had explained that the Burmese were ambitious to expand their empire. They were looking increasingly to the territories of Cachar (a state under British 'protection') and after that, Eastern Bengal (under the British East India Company). On the way to Ava, the Judsons caught sight of a great army, perhaps 30,000 troops. Ann wrote:

> Our fears have been considerably excited for a few days past, on beholding the martial movements of the country. We understand that the Emperor is determined on war with the English, and has ordered an army to proceed with all possible dispatch to Arrakan. Yesterday we passed the head-quarters of the troops, and war boats are continually passing us. We know not what effect this war will have upon our mission, or how much our own lives will be endangered from the suspicion that we are English. But we always have the consolation, that God reigns, and that the greatest, as well as the smallest events are under his direction.[6]

At one point they were threatened by a fleet of Burmese war boats, only escaping when Adoniram explained that they had been invited to Ava by the king himself. The Judsons were absolutely determined not to miss an opportunity to establish a mission in the capital. They proceeded, confident because of the measure of favour won by Adoniram on his last visit to Ava, and confident also because they were American, not British. In fact both these guarantees of protection were hollow. Effectively they were sailing into a trap.

17

War clouds gather (1824)

For the Judsons to proceed to Ava with war about to break out was, with hindsight, a terrible mistake. In a later era, they would certainly have been ordered home by their sending agency. But communications were so slow as to be almost meaningless, and they were left to make their own decisions.

Bad news greeted them when they disembarked at Ava. Dr Jonathan Price said that he, and all other foreigners, were out of favour. There had been a turnover of personnel at court. Those who had favoured the missionaries no longer had much influence. To add to their troubles, the hut that Adoniram had built was not fit to live in. Price's house was so damp that even a few hours spent there brought Ann out in a fever. The Judsons had no option but to stay on the boat until a better shelter could be built on the land they had leased. This took two weeks. When it was completed Adoniram and Ann settled in and made it home.

Ann wrote to her parents from Ava on 10 February 1824:

> On our arrival at Ava, we had more difficulties to encounter,
> and such as we had never before experienced. We had no home,
> no house to shelter us from the burning sun by day, and the
> cold dews at night. Dr. Price had kindly met us on the way, and
> urged our taking residence with him; but his house was in such
> an unfinished state, and the walls so damp, (of brick, and just
> built) that spending two or three hours threw me into a fever,
> and induced me to feel that it would be presumption to remain
> longer. We had but one alternative, to remain in the boat till we
> could build a small house on the spot of ground which the king
> gave Mr. Judson last year. And you will hardly believe it possible,
> for I almost doubt my senses, that in just a fortnight from our
> arrival, we moved into a house built in that time, and which is
> sufficiently large to make us comfortable. It is in a most delightful
> situation, out of the dust of the town, and on the bank of the
> river. The spot of ground given by his majesty is small, being
> only 120 feet long, and 75 wide; but it is our own, and is the most
> healthy situation I have seen. Our house is raised four feet from
> the ground, and consists of three small rooms and a verandah.
>
> I hardly know how we shall bear the hot season, which is just
> commencing, as our house is built of boards, and before night, is
> heated like an oven. Nothing but brick is a shelter from the heat
> of Ava, where the thermometer, even in the shade, frequently
> rises to a hundred and eighty degrees. We have worship every
> evening in Burman, when a number of the natives assemble;
> and every Sabbath Mr. Judson preaches the other side of the
> river, in Dr. Price's house. We feel it an inestimable privilege,

that amid all our discouragements we have the language, and are able constantly to communicate truths which can save the soul.

My female school has already commenced, with three little girls, who are learning to read, sew, etc. Two of them are sisters, and we have named them, Mary and Abby Hasseltine. One of them is to be supported with the money which the 'Judson Association of Bradford Academy' have engaged to collect. They are fine children, and improve as rapidly as any children in the world. Their mother is deranged, and their father gave them to me to educate, so that I have been at no expense for them, excepting their food and clothes. I have already begun to make inquiries for children, and doubt not we shall be directed in regard to our school.

I have not yet been at the palace, the royal family all being absent. They returned to Amarapoora a day or so after our arrival, where they will remain till the new palace in this city is finished, when they will take possession in usual form, and Ava in future will be their residence. My old friend, the lady of the Viceroy of Rangoon, who died in my absence, came to the boat to see me immediately on being informed of my arrival. All her power and distinction ceased at the death of her husband, and she is now only a private woman. She is, however, a very sensible woman, and there is much more hope of her attending to the subject of religion now, than when in public life. I intend to visit her frequently, and make it an object to fix her attention to the subject. In consequence of war with the Bengal government, foreigners are not so much esteemed at court as formerly. I know not what effect this war will have on our mission; but we must leave the event with Him who has hitherto directed us (271–3).

Their situation was vulnerable in the extreme, and yet they do not seem to have realized the danger. Ann was very optimistic when she wrote to Josiah Butterworth on 16 February 1824:

> In a day or two after our arrival, Mr. J. introduced me to Prince M. and his Princess; they treated us with the greatest kindness. The Princess took me into her inner apartments, made me a handsome present, and invited me to visit her frequently, and ordered her cart to be prepared to convey me home. Prince M. is intelligent, desirous of obtaining foreign information, and has for some time been examining the Christian religion! Oh! that a merciful God would enlighten his mind, and make him a real disciple of the blessed Redeemer. I hope to gain some influence over the Princess, and induce her to read the New Testament, which is now in her own language. She is surrounded at all times by twenty or thirty females, and who knows but religious conversation may be blessed to them, though the Princess herself should never be benefited. We have here an uncommon field for usefulness, and if we may only be allowed to remain, there is no doubt but much good would be done. My health has been much improved during my voyages, and I begin to hope that I may last yet some years; but we are, in a literal sense, alone. We have not half the means of obtaining intelligence from our friends as when in Rangoon; and as for society, it is so far out of the question, that we hardly think of mentioning it. Dr. Price is our only missionary associate; but he has married a native wife, and lives the other side of the river. Mr. J. preaches every Sabbath in the Doctor's house, where he has something of a congregation. We also have worship in Burman every evening in our own house, so that a faint ray of light is beginning to appear in this dark city.

Remember me most affectionately to—, whose likeness is now hanging before me, and is almost the only ornament in our little house. Pray kindly write a line to Miss H., of Liverpool, and inform her that the box of articles she forwarded arrived just as I was leaving Calcutta. They were most acceptable, as we have daily occasions for distributing them. Say also that I intend writing to her very soon. Do not forget to pray for

Your most affectionate Friend,

A. H. Judson[1]

Incredibly, even when news broke of the British invasion of Rangoon in May 1824, the Judsons and Price remained in Ava. During the invasion of Rangoon, the Burmese had imprisoned Wade and Hough, but on taking control the English had ordered the release of all prisoners. Jonathan Wade wrote to the missionaries in Calcutta on 15 May 1824:

It is between two and three months since we have received any letter from Mr. Judson, or Dr. Price. It is impossible to predict their fate. We tremble whenever we think of them. We can only pray that God, who has delivered us out of the hands of our cruel enemies, may deliver them also (277).

The Houghs and Wades returned to Bengal. While full-scale war raged between the Burmese and the British, all white-skinned foreigners were immediately suspect. The short-term prospects for mission were bleak. In the long term it was clear to the missionaries that if Burma was defeated by the British and a protectorate set up, then the way would be wide open for Christian mission to resume.

From May 1824 onwards army after army sent out by the Burmese government was defeated by the British. The bewilderment and fury of the Burmese government were intense. They had regarded their armies as invincible. Some treachery must lie behind the disasters; there must be spies at work for the British. Suspicion fell upon all foreigners, and the missionaries were doomed.

For nearly two years there was no news of the Judsons or Price. Their friends and family feared the worst. At last, it was heard that the British army had advanced within forty miles of the capital. The King of Burma realized that further resistance was futile, and that unless peace was made Ava itself would be occupied. He was forced to cede a large portion of Burma to the British, promise a huge amount of money and hand over all foreign prisoners. The Judsons and Price arrived at the British camp on 24 February 1826. But what had happened to them in the intervening two years?

18

'Hand, shrink not': the heart of darkness (1824–1825)

On 23 May 1824, the Judsons and Price heard of the fall of Rangoon to the British. In retrospect, it seems remarkable that they did not seek immediate escape from Ava. However, they still believed that the Burmese would distinguish between British and American citizens and hoped that they would be left alone.

Their closest friend in Ava was a young English merchant, Henry Gouger by name. Prudence should have dictated his escape long before this, but he too had hung on. He was reluctant to abandon the wealth he had accrued. Gouger received an assurance (empty as it turned out) from one of the princes that 'The new foreigners residing at Ava had nothing to do with the war, and should not be molested' (284). The Judsons at first took some comfort from this assurance. But when Gouger and the other two Englishmen then resident in Ava

were imprisoned, the missionaries realized that their situation was untenable. 'We now began to tremble for ourselves,' wrote Ann (285).

Shortly afterwards Price and Judson were interrogated as to their relations with Great Britain. They managed to convince the officials that they were not in the pay of the British at Bengal and were allowed home. But the Burmese then discovered that Gouger had been cashing orders of payment for the missionaries. Although this had been an innocent and routine way of receiving funds via Bengal, it was proof positive to the Burmese that Judson and Price were in the pay of the British and must be spies. The king ordered their immediate arrest. On 8 June 1824 Judson and Price were thrown into the Death Prison, which on account of the unspeakable tortures perpetrated inside was commonly known as 'Hand, shrink not'. They would not know freedom until February 1826.

Ann subsequently wrote a detailed account of the whole ordeal to her brother-in-law, Elnathan Judson.[1]

> On the 8th of June, just as we were preparing for dinner, in rushed an officer holding a black book, with a dozen Burmans, accompanied by *one*, who, from his spotted face, we knew to be an executioner, and a 'son of the prison.' 'Where is the teacher?' was the first inquiry. Mr. Judson presented himself. 'You are called by the king,' said the officer; a form of speech always used when about to arrest a criminal. The spotted man instantly seized Mr. Judson, threw him on the floor, and produced the small cord, the instrument of torture. I caught hold of his arm; 'Stay, (said I,) I will give you money.' 'Take her too,' said the officer; 'she also is a foreigner.' Mr. Judson, with an imploring look, begged they would let me remain till further orders. The scene now was

shocking beyond description. The whole neighbourhood had
collected—the masons at work on the brick house threw down
their tools, and ran—the little Burman children were screaming
and crying—the Bengalee servants stood in amazement at the
indignities offered their master—and the hardened executioner,
with a kind of hellish joy, drew tight the cords, bound Mr. Judson
fast, and dragged him off I knew not whither. In vain I begged
and entreated the spotted face to take the silver, and loosen the
ropes; but he spurned my offers, and immediately departed. I
gave the money, however, to Moung Ing to follow after, to make
some further attempt to mitigate the torture of Mr. Judson;
but instead of succeeding, when a few rods from the house, the
unfeeling wretches again threw their prisoner on the ground, and
drew the cords still tighter, so as almost to prevent respiration.

The officer and his gang proceeded on to the court house, where
the governor of the city and officers were collected, one of whom
read the order of the king, to commit Mr. Judson to the death
prison, into which he was soon hurled, the door closed—and
Moung Ing saw no more. What a night was now before me! I
retired into my room, and endeavoured to obtain consolation
from committing my case to God, and imploring fortitude and
strength to suffer whatever awaited me. But the consolation of
retirement was not long allowed me, for the magistrate of the
place had come into the verandah, and continually called me to
come out, and submit to his examination. But previously to going
out, I destroyed all my letters, journals, and writings of every kind,
lest they should disclose the fact, that we had correspondents
in England, and had minuted down every occurrence since our
arrival in the country. When this work of destruction was finished,
I went out and submitted to the examination of the magistrate,

who inquired very minutely of every thing I knew; then ordered the gates of the compound to be shut, no person to be allowed to go in or out, placed a guard of ten ruffians, to whom he gave a strict charge to keep me safe, and departed.

It was now dark. I retired to an inner room with my four little Burman girls, and barred the doors. The guard instantly ordered me to unbar the doors and come out, or they would break the house down. I obstinately refused to obey, and endeavoured to intimidate them by threatening to complain of their conduct to higher authorities on the morrow. Finding me resolved in disregarding their orders, they took the two Bengalee servants, and confined them in the stocks, in a very painful position. I could not endure this; but called the head man to a window, and promised to make them all a present in the morning, if they would relieve the servants. After much debate and many severe threatenings, they consented, but seemed resolved to annoy me as much as possible. My unprotected desolate state, my entire uncertainty of the fate of Mr. Judson, and the dreadful carousings and almost diabolical language of the guard, all conspired to make it by far the most distressing night I have ever passed. You may well imagine, my dear brother, that sleep was a stranger to my eyes, and peace and composure to my mind.

The next morning, I sent Moung Ing, to ascertain the situation of your brother, and give him some food, if still living. He soon returned with the intelligence, that Mr. Judson, and all the white foreigners, were confined in the *death prison*, with three pair of iron fetters each, and fastened to a long pole to prevent their moving! The point of my anguish now was, that I was a prisoner myself, and could make no efforts for the release of the

Missionaries. I begged and entreated the magistrate to allow me to go to some member of government to state my case; but he said he did not dare to consent, for fear I should escape. I next wrote a note to one of the king's sisters, with whom I had been intimate, requesting her to use her influence for the release of the teachers. The note was returned with this message—She 'did not understand it,'—which was a polite refusal to interfere; though I afterwards ascertained, that she had an anxious desire to assist us, but dared not on account of the queen. The day dragged heavily away, and another dreadful night was before me. I endeavoured to soften the feelings of the guard, by giving them tea and segars for the night; so they allowed me to remain inside of my room, without threatening as they did the night before. But the idea of your brother being stretched on the bare floor in irons and confinement, haunted my mind like a spectre, and prevented my obtaining any quiet sleep, though nature was almost exhausted.

On the third day, I sent a message to the governor of the city, who has the entire direction of prison affairs, to allow me to visit him with a present. This had the desired effect; and he immediately sent orders to the guards, to permit my going into town. The governor received me pleasantly, and asked me what I wanted. I stated to him the situation of the foreigners, and particularly that of the teachers, who were Americans, and had nothing to do with the war. He told me it was not in his power to release them from prison or irons, but that he could make their situation more comfortable; there was his head officer, with whom I must consult, relative to the means. The officer, who proved to be one of the city writers, and whose countenance at the first glance presented the most perfect assemblage of all the evil passions attached to human nature, took me aside, and endeavoured to

convince me, that myself, as well as the prisoners, was entirely
at his disposal—that our future comfort must depend on my
liberality in regard to presents—and that these must be made
in a private way, and unknown to any officer in the government!
What must I do, said I, to obtain a mitigation of the present
sufferings of the two teachers? 'Pay to me,' said he, 'two hundred
tickals, (about a hundred dollars,) two pieces of fine cloth, and
two pieces of handkerchiefs.' I had taken money with me in the
morning, our house being two miles from the prison—I could
not easily return. This I offered to the writer, and begged he
would not insist on the other articles, as they were not in my
possession. He hesitated for some time, but fearing to lose the
sight of so much money, he concluded to take it, promising to
relieve the teachers from their most painful situation.

I then procured an order from the governor, for my admittance
into prison; but the sensations produced by meeting your brother
in that *wretched, horrid* situation, and the affecting scene which
ensued, I will not attempt to describe. Mr. Judson crawled to
the door of the prison—for I was never allowed to enter—gave
me some directions relative to his release; but before we could
make any arrangements, I was ordered to depart, by those iron-
hearted jailers, who could not endure to see us enjoy the poor
consolation of meeting in that miserable place. In vain I pleaded
the order from the governor for my admittance; they again harshly
repeated, 'Depart, or we will pull you out.' The same evening, the
Missionaries, together with the other foreigners, who paid an
equal sum, were taken out of the common prison, and confined
in an open shed in the prison enclosure. Here I was allowed to
send them food, and mats to sleep on; but was not permitted to
enter again for several days (286–90).

Ann was fully occupied every day for the next seven months. Prisoners were completely dependent on friends and relations for food, so much of her time was spent attempting to get meals into the prison. Adoniram later recollected one such visit for Emily, his third wife, and she described it as follows:

> His food was such as Mrs. Judson could provide. Sometimes it came regularly, and sometimes they went very hungry. Sometimes, for weeks together, they had no food but rice, savoured with ngapee—a certain preparation of fish, not always palatable to foreigners. But once, when a term of unusual quiet gave her time for the softer and more homely class of loving thoughts, Mrs. Judson made a great effort to surprise her husband with something that should remind him of home. She planned and laboured, until, by the aid of buffalo beef and plantains, she actually concocted a mince-pie. Unfortunately, as she thought, she could not go in person to the prison that day; and the dinner was brought by smiling Moung Ing, who seemed aware that some mystery must be wrapped up in that peculiar preparation of meat and fruit, though he had never seen the well-spread boards of Plymouth and Bradford. But the pretty little artifice only added another pang to a heart whose susceptibilities were as quick and deep, as, in the sight of the world, they were silent. When his wife had visited him in prison, and borne taunts and insults with and for him, they could be brave together; when she had stood up like an enchantress, winning the hearts of high and low, making savage gaolers, and scarcely less savage nobles, weep; or moved, protected by her own dignity and sublimity of purpose, like a queen along the streets, his heart had throbbed with proud admiration; and he was almost able to thank God for the trials which had made a character so intrinsically noble

shine forth with such peculiar brightness. But in this simple, homelike act, this little unpretending effusion of a loving heart, there was something so touching, so unlike the part she had just been acting, and yet so illustrative of what she really was, that he bowed his head upon his knees, and the tears flowed down to the chains about his ankles.[2]

The other vital ministry Ann performed was to preserve Adoniram's precious manuscript of the translation of the New Testament. She buried it in the garden as a short-term expedient, but fearing that it would rot, she packed it up into a pillow and brought it into the prison for Adoniram. He was able to keep it for the duration of his imprisonment in Ava. The rest of her time she spent in visiting everyone she could think of in Ava, pleading for the release of her husband and Dr Price. She used her charm to the utmost, and was liberal with bribes, but the inexorable advance of the British troops meant that her efforts seemed futile. In fact, it was probably her intercessions that spared the lives of the missionaries, and certainly their chances of survival were greatly enhanced by her success in getting them moved at times out of the filthy and grossly overcrowded inner prison into the yard. She found herself subject to continual harassment from lesser officials, who saw opportunities to enrich themselves by exploiting her vulnerable situation. Summoned at least once for interrogation herself, she still took the risk of continually visiting individuals from the government and the royal family:

For the seven following months, hardly a day passed, that I did not visit some one of the members of government, or branches of the royal family, in order to gain their influence in our behalf; but the only benefit resulting was, their encouraging promises preserved us from despair, and induced a hope of the

speedy termination of our difficulties, which enabled us to bear
our distresses better than we otherwise should have done. I
ought, however, to mention, that by my repeated visits to the
different members of government, I gained several friends, who
were ready to assist me with articles of food, though in a private
manner, and who used their influence in the palace to destroy
the impression of our being in any way engaged in the present
war. But no one dared to speak a word to the king or queen in
favour of a foreigner, while there were such continual reports of
the success of the English arms.

During these seven months, the continual extortions and
oppressions to which your brother, and the other white prisoners,
were subject, are indescribable. Sometimes sums of money were
demanded, sometimes pieces of cloth, and handkerchiefs; at
other times, an order would be issued, that the white foreigners
should not speak to each other, or have any communication with
their friends without. Then again, the servants were forbidden
to carry in their food, without an extra fee. Sometimes, for days
and days together, I could not go into the prison, till after dark,
when I had two miles to walk, in returning to the house. O how
many, many times, have I returned from that dreary prison at nine
o'clock at night, solitary and worn out with fatigue and anxiety,
and thrown myself down in that same rocking chair which you
and Deacon L. provided for me in Boston, and endeavoured
to invent some new scheme for the release of the prisoners.
Sometimes, for a moment or two, my thoughts would glance
toward America, and my beloved friends there—but for nearly
a year and a half, so entirely engrossed was every thought with
present scenes and sufferings, that I seldom reflected on a single

occurrence of my former life, or recollected that I had a friend
in existence out of Ava.

You, my dear brother, who know my strong attachment to my
friends, and how much pleasure I have hitherto experienced
from retrospect, can judge from the above circumstances, how
intense were my sufferings. But the point, the acme of my
distress, consisted in the awful uncertainty of our final fate. My
prevailing opinion was, that my husband would suffer violent
death; and that I should, of course, become a slave, and languish
out a miserable though short existence, in the tyrannic hands of
some unfeeling monster. But the consolations of religion, in these
trying circumstances, were neither 'few nor small.' It taught me
to look beyond this world, to that rest, that peaceful happy rest,
where Jesus reigns, and oppression never enters (295–6).

Supreme power at this time lay with Bandoola, the commander of
the Burman forces. With the audacity born of despair, Ann decided to
go direct to him and plead on her husband's behalf. When that failed
she focused her efforts on the Governor of Ava, and with him her
legendary grace and charm evidently had great effect. He allowed her
to take steps to alleviate conditions for her husband, but was unable
to secure his release:

From this time, we gave up all idea of being released from
prison, till the termination of the war; but I was still obliged to
visit constantly some of the members of government, with little
presents; particularly the governor of the city, for the purpose
of making the situation of the prisoners tolerable. I generally
spent the greater part of every other day at the governor's house,
giving him all the information relative to American manners,

customs, government, etc. He used to be so much gratified with my communications, as to feel greatly disappointed, if any occurrence prevented my spending the usual hours at his house.

Some months after your brother's imprisonment, I was permitted to make a little bamboo room in the prison enclosures, where he could be much by himself, and where I was sometimes allowed to spend two or three hours. It so happened that the two months he occupied this place, was the coldest part of the year, when he would have suffered much in the open shed he had previously occupied (297–8).

Adoniram was not the only prisoner to owe his survival to Ann. One of his fellow-prisoners, an Englishman, later described the 'ministering angel' who supplied him and other prisoners with food and clothes and constantly interceded on their behalf:

... though living at a distance of two miles from our prison, without any means of conveyance, and very feeble in health, [she] forgot her own comfort and infirmity, and almost every day visited us, sought out and administered to our wants, and contributed in every way to alleviate our misery ... Besides all this, it was unquestionably owing, in a chief degree, to the repeated eloquence and forcible appeals of Mrs Judson, that the untutored Burman was finally made willing to secure the welfare and happiness of his country by a sincere peace.[3]

But by the beginning of 1825 Ann realized that she could not continue the prison visits much longer. Their child would arrive at any time now. When little Roger had been born at Rangoon she had

at least had Adoniram with her. Now she would be alone. Prospects for the family could not have seemed worse.

19

Maria (1825)

On 26 January 1825 Ann gave birth to a little girl. She was called Maria Elizabeth Butterworth Judson, after the kind friend in England who had shown such generosity and love. After a confinement of about three weeks Ann brought the little one to the prison to meet her father. As usual she wore the native Burman dress, and Adoniram later described this meeting to Emily who depicted the scene as follows:

Behold her, then—her dark curls carefully straightened, drawn back from her forehead, and a fragrant cocoa-blossom, drooping like a white plume from the knot upon the crown; her saffron vest thrown open to display the folds of crimson beneath; and a rich silken skirt, wrapped closely about her fine figure, parting at the ankle, and sloping back upon the floor. The clothing of the feet was not Burman, for the native sandal could not be worn except upon a bare foot. Behold her standing in the doorway (for she was never permitted to enter the prison), her little blue-eyed

blossom wailing, as it almost always did, upon her bosom, and the chained father crawling forth to the meeting![1]

Adoniram composed a twenty-four-verse poem after this first glimpse of baby Maria. These nine verses extracted from the poem give some hint of the depth of his grief; he was unable even to hold his little daughter, and humanly speaking he had no prospect of ever providing for her:

> *Lines addressed to an Infant Daughter, twenty days old, in the condemned Prison at Ava*

Sleep, darling infant, sleep,
Hushed on thy mother's breast;
Let no rude sound of clanking chains
Disturb thy balmy rest.

Sleep, darling infant, sleep;
Blest that thou canst not know
The pangs that rend thy parents' hearts,
The keenness of their woe …

Why ope' thy little eyes?
What would my darling see?
Thy sorrowing mother's bending form?
Thy father's agony?

Wouldst view this drear abode,
Where fettered felons lie,
And wonder that thy father here
Should as a felon sigh?

Wouldst mark the dreadful sights,
Which stoutest hearts appal—
The stocks, the cord, the fatal sword,
The torturing iron mall?

No, darling infant, no!
Thou seest them not at all;
Thou only mark'st the rays of light
Which flicker on the wall ...

Go, darling infant, go;
Thine hour has passed away;
The jailer's harsh, discordant voice
Forbids thy longer stay ...

There is a God on high,
The glorious King of kings;
'Tis He to whom thy mother prays,
Whose love she sits and sings ...

And to that gracious God
My darling I commend;
Be Thou the helpless orphan's stay,
Her Father and her Friend ...

To Maria Eliza Butterworth Judson, born at Ava, January 26,
1825.[2]

Ann, now carrying baby Maria everywhere she went, resumed her round of visiting the prison and calling on any who might be able to help. She found that her time of confinement meant that she had

lost a measure of the favour she had gained with the Governor of
Ava, but she set about regaining influence. In the event it was only
the governor's regard for Ann that stood between the missionaries
and death. When orders came from above for him to kill the foreign
prisoners he resorted to having them hidden within the inner part of
the prison and secured with five pairs of fetters, as Ann later described
to Elnathan:

> After the birth of your little niece, I was unable to visit the
> prison and governor as before, and found I had lost considerable
> influence, previously gained; for he was not so forward to hear
> my petitions when any difficulty occurred, as he formerly had
> been. When Maria was nearly two months old, her father one
> morning sent me word that he and all the white prisoners were
> put into the inner prison, in five pairs of fetters each; that this
> little room had been torn down, and his mat, pillow, etc. been
> taken by the jailers. This was to me a dreadful shock, as I thought
> at once it was only a prelude to greater evils.
>
> I should have mentioned before this, the defeat of Bandoola,
> his escape to Danooboo, the complete destruction of his army
> and loss of ammunition, and the consternation this intelligence
> produced at court. The English army had left Rangoon, and were
> advancing towards Prome, when these severe measures were
> taken with the prisoners.
>
> I went immediately to the governor's house. He was not at
> home, but had ordered his wife to tell me, when I came, not to ask
> to have the additional fetters taken off, or the prisoners released,
> for *it could not be done*. I went to the prison gate, but was forbid
> to enter. All was still as death—not a white face to be seen, or a

vestige of Mr. J.'s little room remaining. I was determined to see the governor, and know the cause of this additional oppression; and for this purpose returned into the town the same evening, at an hour I knew he would be at home. He was in his audience-room, and as I entered, looked up without speaking, but exhibited a mixture of shame and affected anger in his countenance. I began by saying, Your lordship has hitherto treated us with the kindness of a father. Our obligations to you are very great. We have looked to you for protection from oppression and cruelty. You have in many instances mitigated the sufferings of those unfortunate, though innocent beings, committed to your charge. You have promised me particularly, that you would stand by me to the last, and though you should receive an order from the king, you would not put Mr. J. to death. What crime has he committed to deserve such additional punishment?—The old man's hard heart was melted, for he wept like a child. 'I pity you Tsa-yar-ga-dau, (a name by which he always called me) I knew you would make me feel; I therefore forbade your application. But you must believe me when I say, I do not wish to increase the sufferings of the prisoners. When I am ordered to execute them, the least that I can do, is to put them out of sight. I will now tell you (continued he) what I have never told you before, that three times I have received intimations from the queen's brother, to assassinate all the white prisoners privately; but I would not do it. And I now repeat it, though I execute all the others, I will never execute your husband. But I cannot release him from his present confinement, and you must not ask it.' I had never seen him manifest so much feeling, or so resolute in denying me a favour, which circumstance was an additional reason for thinking dreadful scenes were before us.

The situation of the prisoners was now distressing beyond description. It was at the commencement of the hot season. There were above a hundred prisoners shut up in one room, without a breath of air excepting from the cracks in the boards. I sometimes obtained permission to go to the door for five minutes, when my heart sickened at the wretchedness exhibited. The white prisoners, from incessant perspiration and loss of appetite, looked more like the dead than the living. I made daily applications to the governor, offering him money, which he refused; but all that I gained, was permission for the foreigners to eat their food outside, and this continued but a short time …

After continuing in the inner prison for more than a month, your brother was taken with a fever. I felt assured that he would not live long, unless removed from that noisome place. To effect this, and in order to be near the prison, I removed from our house, and put up a small bamboo room in the governor's enclosure, which was nearly opposite the prison gate. Here I incessantly begged the governor to give me an order to take Mr. J. out of the large prison, and place him in a more comfortable situation; and the old man, being worn out with my entreaties, at length gave me an order in an official form; and also gave orders to the head jailer, to allow me to go in and out all times of the day, to administer medicines, etc. I now felt happy indeed, and had Mr. J. instantly removed into a little bamboo hovel, so low, that neither of us could stand upright—but a palace in comparison with the place he had left' (298–301).

Ann could congratulate herself that she had done everything humanly possible to alleviate Adoniram's suffering. But once again the progress of the war set in train dire consequences for the foreign

prisoners. On 1 April 1825 the Burmese commander Bandoola was killed in action. The king and his government were utterly bewildered as to what to do next, and the ordinary people who had borne all of the cost of the war so far whispered of rebellion.

At this time one of the king's advisers, the Pakan Woon, came up with a new scheme to defeat the British. He had been disgraced and thrown into the Death Prison along with the foreigners, but he was now released and put in charge of the army. Pakan Woon was, of all Burmans, most viciously opposed to all foreigners, and once he was in power again the death of Adoniram, Jonathan and the others seemed inevitable. He moved swiftly, but the prisoners were not to be killed just yet. He ordered their immediate removal to his home village, Oung-pen-la. There they were to be held, until he was ready to advance against the British. Rumour came that the foreigners would then be offered up as a sacrifice to bring good fortune in the battle, probably by being buried alive before the advancing Burman army.

Their forced march to Oung-pen-la took place on 2 May 1825. The governor, showing as much kindness as he could in the circumstances, ensured that Ann did not witness the brutality of their removal. Knowing that the men were doomed, he then advised her to leave them to their fate, and look after herself. Ann of course ignored this advice, and determined to discover where the prisoners had been taken:

> Notwithstanding the order the governor had given for my admittance into prison, it was with the greatest difficulty that I could persuade the under jailer to open the gate. I used to carry Mr. J's food myself for the sake of getting in, and would then

remain an hour or two unless driven out. We had been in this comfortable situation but two or three days, when one morning, having carried in Mr. Judson's breakfast, which in consequence of fever he was unable to take, I remained longer than usual, when the governor in great haste sent for me. I promised him to return as soon as I had ascertained the governor's will, he being much alarmed at this unusual message. I was very agreeably disappointed, when the governor informed me, that he only wished to consult me about his watch, and seemed unusually pleasant and conversable. I found afterwards, that his only object was, to detain me until the dreadful scene about to take place in the prison was over. For when I left him to go to my room, one of the servants came running, and with a ghastly countenance informed me, that all the white prisoners were carried away. I would not believe the report, and instantly went back to the governor, who said, he had just heard of it, but did not wish to tell me. I hastily ran into the street, hoping to get a glimpse of them before they were out of sight, but in this was disappointed. I ran first into one street, then another, inquiring of all I met, but no one would answer me. At length an old woman told me, the white prisoners had gone towards the little river; for they were to be carried to Amarapoora. I then ran to the banks of the little river, about half a mile, but saw them not, and concluded the old woman had deceived me. Some of the friends of the foreigners went to the place of execution, but found them not. I then returned to the governor, to try to discover the cause of their removal, and the probability of their future fate. The old man assured me that he was ignorant of the intention of government to remove the foreigners till that morning: That since I went out he had learned, that the prisoners were to be sent to Amarapoora; but for what purpose, he knew not. 'I will send off a man immediately,' said he,

'to see what is to be done with them. You can do nothing more for your husband,' continued he, *'take care of yourself.'* With a heavy heart, I went to my room, and having no hope to excite me to exertion, I sunk almost into despair. For several days previous, I had been actively engaged in building my own little room, and making my hovel comfortable. My thoughts had been almost entirely occupied in contriving means to get into prison. But now I looked towards the gate with a kind of melancholy feeling, but no wish to enter. All was the stillness of death, no preparation of your brother's food, no expectation of meeting him at the usual dinner hour, all my employment, all my occupations seemed to have ceased, and I had nothing left but the dreadful recollection that Mr. Judson was carried off, I knew not whither.—It was one of the most insupportable days I have ever passed. Towards night, however, I came to the determination to set off the next morning for Amarapoora; and for this purpose was obliged to go to our house out of town.

Never before have I suffered so much from fear in traversing the streets of Ava. The last word of the governor, 'Take care of yourself,' made me suspect there was some design with which I was unacquainted. I saw, also, he was afraid to have me go into the street, and advised me to wait till dark, when he would send me a cart, and a man to open the gates. I took two or three trunks of the most valuable articles, together with the medicine chest, to deposit in the house of the governor; and after committing the house and premises to our faithful Moung Ing and a Bengal servant, who continued with us, (though we were unable to pay his wages) I took leave, as I then thought probable, of our house in Ava for ever (301–3).

Ann then heard from a servant that the white prisoners had been sent to Amarapoora, and were to be sent on the next day to some place further off—where, he did not know. Ann determined to follow, but her journey in pursuit of Adoniram and the prisoners was all the more appalling because she was carrying baby Maria into the unknown:

> The next morning, I obtained a pass from government, and with my little Maria, who was then only three months old, Mary and Abby Hasseltine, [two of the Burman children] and our Bengalee cook, who was the only one of the party that could afford me any assistance, I set off for Amarapoora. The day was dreadfully hot, but we obtained a covered boat, in which we were tolerably comfortable, till within two miles of the government house. I then procured a cart; but the violent motion, together with the dreadful heat and dust, made me almost distracted. But what was my disappointment on my arriving at the court house, to find that the prisoners had been sent on two hours before, and that I must go in that uncomfortable mode four miles further with little Maria in my arms, whom I had held all the way from Ava. The cart-man refused to go any further; and after waiting an hour in the burning sun, I procured another, and set off for that never to be forgotten place, Oung-pen-la. I obtained a guide from the governor, and was conducted directly to the prison yard. But what a scene of wretchedness was presented to my view! The prison was an old shattered building, without a roof; the fence was entirely destroyed; eight or ten Burmans were on the top of the building, trying to make something like a shelter with leaves; while under a little low projection outside the prison, sat the foreigners, chained together two and two, almost dead with suffering and fatigue. The first words of your brother were,

'Why have you come? I hoped you would not follow, for you cannot live here' (304).

Ann had achieved her immediate objective. She had found Adoniram alive.

20

Six months at Oung-pen-la (1825)

A doniram was half dead, and appalled to see Ann in this desolate
spot. Where would she stay? What would become of the baby?
Ann's narrative continued:

> It was now dark. I had no refreshment for the suffering prisoners,
> or for myself, as I had expected to procure all that was necessary
> at the market of Amarapoora, and I had no shelter for the night.
> I asked one of the jailers if I might put up a little bamboo house
> near the prison; he said no, it was not customary. I then begged
> he would procure for me a shelter for the night, when on the
> morrow I could find some place to live in. He took me to his
> house, in which there were only two small rooms, one in which
> he and his family lived, the other, which was then half full of
> grain, he offered to me; and in that little filthy place, I spent the
> next six months of wretchedness. I procured some half boiled
> water, instead of my tea, and worn out with fatigue, laid myself

down on a mat spread over the paddy, and endeavoured to obtain a little refreshment from sleep (304–5).

The next morning Ann made her way to the miserable group of prisoners. Adoniram told her of the horrors of their journey to Oung-pen-la. Ann gave this graphic description to Adoniram's brother, Elnathan:

> As soon as I had gone out at the call of the governor, one of the jailers rushed into Mr. J.'s little room—roughly seized him by the arm—pulled him out—stripped him of all his clothes, excepting shirt and pantaloons—took his shoes, hat, and all his bedding—tore off all his chains—tied a rope round his waist, and dragged him to the court house, where the other prisoners had previously been taken. They were then tied two and two, and delivered into the hands of the Lamine Woon, who went on before them on horseback, while his slaves drove the prisoners, one of the slaves holding the rope which connected two of them together. It was in May, one of the hottest months in the year, and eleven o'clock in the day, so that the sun was intolerable indeed. They had proceeded only half a mile, when your brother's feet became blistered, and so great was his agony, even at this early period, that as they were crossing the little river, he ardently longed to throw himself into the water to be free from misery. But the sin attached to such an act alone prevented. They had then eight miles to walk. The sand and gravel were like burning coals to the feet of the prisoners, which soon became perfectly destitute of skin, and in that wretched state they were goaded on by their unfeeling drivers. Mr. J's debilitated state, in consequence of fever, and having taken no food that morning, rendered him

less capable of bearing such hardships than the other prisoners (305–6).

One of the prisoners collapsed and died shortly after their arrival at the court house at Amarapoora. There were still four miles to go, but the prisoners could not move. They were allowed to crawl into a shed for the night, and the next day a cart took them on to Oung-pen-la. Rumours circulating back in Ava to the effect that they were to be burned alive on arrival, and so all began to prepare for death. Only when some of the guards began to attempt to repair the dilapidated old hut which acted as the prison did they realize that they did not face imminent death.

It was only an hour or two after their arrival that Ann had arrived with her baby Maria, her two little adopted Burmese girls Mary and Abby and her Bengali cook. None of them knew the fate of the precious New Testament manuscript. In fact the faithful Moung Ing had gone to the prison after the foreign prisoners had been removed to see if he could recover any of Adoniram's possessions. He had picked up the hard, shabby pillow, and thus the fruit of Adoniram's ten years of labour was preserved.[1] Moung Ing watched over the house in Ava, and the manuscript, during the miserable six-month imprisonment at Oung-pen-la.

Ann now had to try to settle into some kind of routine, make a home of some sort for the baby and the two little Burmese girls with her and provide meals for Adoniram. She described the next few months to Elnathan:

> The next morning I arose and endeavoured to find something like food. But there was no market, and nothing to be procured.

One of Dr. Price's friends, however, brought some cold rice and vegetable curry from Amarapoora, which, together with a cup of tea from Mr. Lansago, answered for the breakfast of the prisoners; and for dinner, we made a curry of dried salt fish, which a servant of Mr. Gouger had brought. All the money I could command in the world, I had brought with me, secreted about my person; so you may judge what our prospects were, in case the war should continue long. But our heavenly Father was better to us than our fears; for notwithstanding the constant extortions of the jailers during the whole six months we were at Oung-pen-la, and the frequent straits to which we were brought, we never really suffered for the want of money, though frequently for want of provisions, which were not procurable. Here at this place my personal bodily sufferings commenced. While your brother was confined in the city prison, I had been allowed to remain in our house, in which I had many conveniences left, and my health had continued good beyond all expectations. But now I had not a single article of convenience—not even a chair or seat of any kind, excepting a bamboo floor. The very morning after my arrival, Mary Hasseltine was taken with the small pox, the natural way. She, though very young, was the only assistant I had in taking care of little Maria. But she now required all the time I could spare from Mr. Judson, whose fever still continued in prison, and whose feet were so dreadfully mangled, that for several days he was unable to move. I knew not what to do, for I could procure no assistance from the neighbourhood, or medicine for the sufferers, but was all day long going backwards and forwards from the house to the prison, with little Maria in my arms. Sometimes I was greatly relieved by leaving her, for an hour, when asleep, by the side of her father, while I returned to the house to look after Mary, whose fever ran so high as to

produce delirium. She was so completely covered with the small pox, that there was no distinction in the pustules. As she was in the same small room with myself, I knew Maria would take it; I therefore inoculated her from another child,[2] before Mary's had arrived at such a state as to be infectious. At the same time I inoculated Abbey, and the jailer's children, who all had it so lightly as hardly to interrupt their play. But the inoculation in the arm of my poor little Maria did not take—she caught it off Mary, and had it the natural way. She was then only three months and a half old, and had been a most healthy child; but it was about three months before she perfectly recovered from the effects of this dreadful disorder.

You will recollect I never had the small pox, but was vaccinated previously to leaving America. In consequence of being for so long a time constantly exposed, I had nearly a hundred pustules formed, though no previous symptoms of fever, etc. The jailer's children having had the small pox so lightly, in consequence of inoculation, my fame was spread all over the village, and every child, young and old, who had not previously had it, was brought for inoculation. And though I knew nothing about the disorder, or the mode of treating it, I inoculated them all with a needle, and told them to take care of their diet,—all the instructions I could give them. Mr. Judson's health was gradually restored, and he found himself much more comfortably situated, than when in the city prison.

The prisoners were at first chained two and two; but as soon as the jailers could obtain chains sufficient, they were separated, and each prisoner had but one pair. The prison was repaired, a new fence made, and a large airy shed erected in front of the

prison, where the prisoners were allowed to remain during the day, though locked up in the little close prison at night. All the children recovered from the small pox; but my watchings and fatigue, together with my miserable food, and more miserable lodgings, brought on one of the diseases of the country, which is almost always fatal to foreigners. My constitution seemed destroyed, and in a few days I became so weak as to be hardly able to walk to Mr. Judson's prison. In this debilitated state, I set off in a cart for Ava, to procure medicines, and some suitable food, leaving the cook to supply my place. I reached the house in safety, and for two or three days the disorder seemed at a stand: after which it attacked me so violently, that I had no hopes of recovery left—and my only anxiety now was, to return to Oung-pen-la to die near the prison. It was with the greatest difficulty that I obtained the medicine chest from the governor, and then had no one to administer medicine. I however got at the laudanum,[3] and by taking two drops at a time for several hours, it so far checked the disorder, as to enable me to get on board a boat, though so weak that I could not stand, and again set off for Oung-pen-la. The last four miles was in that painful conveyance, the cart, and in the midst of the rainy season, when the mud almost buries the oxen. You may form some idea of a Burmese cart, when I tell you their wheels are not constructed like ours, but are simply round thick planks with a hole in the middle, through which a pole that supports the body is thrust.

I just reached Oung-pen-la when my strength seemed entirely exhausted. The good native cook came out to help me into the house; but so altered and emaciated was my appearance, that the poor fellow burst into tears at the first sight. I crawled on to the mat in the little room, to which I was confined for more than

two months, and never perfectly recovered, until I came to the English camp. At this period, when I was unable to take care of myself, or look after Mr. Judson, we must both have died had it not been for the faithful and affectionate care of our Bengalee cook. A common Bengalee cook will do nothing but the simple business of cooking: But he seemed to forget his cast, and almost his own wants, in his efforts to serve us. He would provide, cook, and carry your brother's food, and then return and take care of me. I have frequently known him not to taste of food till near night, in consequence of having to go so far for wood and water, and in order to have Mr. Judson's dinner ready at the usual hour. He never complained, never asked for his wages, and never for a moment hesitated to go any where, or to perform any act we required. I take great pleasure in speaking of the faithful conduct of this servant, who is still with us, and I trust has been well rewarded for his services.

Our dear little Maria was the greatest sufferer at this time, my illness depriving her of her usual nourishment, and neither a nurse nor a drop of milk could be procured in the village. By making presents to the jailers, I obtained leave for Mr. Judson to come out of prison [in fetters] and take the little emaciated creature around the village, to beg a little nourishment from those mothers who had young children. Her cries in the night were heart-rending, when it was impossible to supply her wants. I now began to think the very afflictions of Job had come upon me. When in health I could bear the various trials and vicissitudes, through which I was called to pass. But to be confined with sickness, and unable to assist those who were so dear to me, when in distress, was almost too much for me to bear: and had it not been for the consolations of religion, and an assured conviction

that every additional trial was ordered by infinite love and mercy, I must have sunk under my accumulated sufferings. Sometimes our jailers seemed a little softened at our distress, and for several days together allowed Mr. Judson to come to the house, which was to me an unspeakable consolation. Then again they would be as iron-hearted in their demands, as though we were free from sufferings, and in affluent circumstances. The annoyance, the extortions and oppressions to which we were subject, during our six months' residence in Oung-pen-la, are beyond enumeration or description (307–11).

At length some really good news signalled that this miserable existence would some time come to an end. The king had at length tired of the overweening ambition of Pakan Woon. He had him dragged from his presence by his hair and then trampled to death by elephants. The prisoners at Oung-pen-la now knew that their lives were more or less secure. Once the Burmans realized they had no chance of defeating the British, they would have to rely on diplomacy to negotiate the most favourable possible settlement. The Europeans in captivity at Oung-pen-la were the only people in the world who were fluent in both English and Burmese and who could conduct such negotiations. Thus, on 5 November, Judson was released from his leg-irons and ordered to attend formal negotiations as a translator.

The jailers saw one last chance to exploit the miserable situation of the Judsons. They said that no order had come through for Ann's release. She could not leave! The Judsons pleaded in vain that Ann had only ever come to Oung-pen-la voluntarily, that she had never been imprisoned. She was only allowed to leave the village after she had handed over every item of food in their possession.

On their arrival back in Ava, Ann was allowed to go home, but Adoniram was taken to prison. No chances were to be taken; he was

far too valuable to lose. The next day Adoniram was allowed a very brief visit home to pick up food and clothing, when he would have had the joy of realizing that his precious manuscript was safe.

He was then sent up the river to Maloun for six tedious weeks of translation work. Much of that time he was sick with a fever. Apart from being free from leg-irons and from the torments of his jailers, he suffered as much as he had done during his imprisonment. And if he had known of what Ann was suffering during his absence he would have been even more unhappy.

21

Free at last (1826)

The months of misery at Oung-pen-la had taken their inevitable
toll on both Ann and Adoniram. Both succumbed to tropical
fever. No communication between them was possible, so neither knew
of the suffering of the other. Ann later summarized the events of the
next six weeks in a letter to Mrs Deakin:

> He arrived at the Burmese camp in two days, where he was
> kept a close prisoner, without fetters, for six weeks, almost in
> a state of starvation. Soon after his departure for the camp, as
> though my sufferings had not reached their height, I was taken
> with the spotted fever. I knew from the symptoms of the disease
> its dangerous nature, and without any medical attendance or
> scarcely any assistance, I concluded at once it would be fatal.
> But before I could sufficiently command my feelings 'to set my
> house in order' and dispose of my little Maria, I lost my reason,
> and was insensible to all around me. But my heavenly Father
> forsook me not in this wretched situation. Just at this period,

Dr. Price was released from prison, and obtained leave to visit me. He said my case was almost helpless, but had recourse to the most energetic means, which were blessed to my recovery. My hair was shaven off my head, my head and feet were covered with blisters, and every measure taken to recover my reason. A Bengali servant, my only attendant, told me my fever had run seventeen days, five or six of which I was insensible, and refused all nourishment. My recovery seemed to myself and all around me a perfect miracle.[1]

Once the translating duties were done, Adoniram nearly ended up back in captivity at Oung-pen-la because of official incompetence. He had been sent back to Ava from Maloun with the covering message: 'We have no further use for Yoodathan [Judson], we therefore send him back to the Golden City.' On his arrival at the Ava court-house no one recognized him, or knew what do with him. The official in charge asked where he had been before the assignment at Maloun. 'Oung-pen-la' was the answer—so Judson was ordered back there! On hearing of this, although critically ill, Ann managed to get a message to the governor pleading for help:

While in this weak, debilitated state, the servant who had followed your brother to the Burmese camp, came in, and informed me that his master had arrived, and was conducted to the court house in town. I sent off a Burman to watch the movements of government, and to ascertain, if possible, in what way Mr. Judson was to be disposed of. He soon returned with the sad intelligence, that he saw Mr. Judson go out of the palace yard, accompanied by two or three Burmans, who conducted him to one of the prisons, and that it was reported in town, that he was to be sent back to the Oung-pen-la prison. I was too weak

to bear ill tidings of any kind; but a shock so dreadful as this, almost annihilated me. For some time, I could hardly breathe; but at last gained sufficient composure to despatch Moung Ing to our friend, the governor of the north gate, and begged him to make *one more effort* for the release of Mr. Judson, and prevent his being sent back to the country prison, where I knew he must suffer much, as I could not follow. Moung Ing then went in search of Mr. Judson; and it was nearly dark, when he found him in the interior of an obscure prison. I had sent food early in the afternoon, but being unable to find him, the bearer had returned with it, which added another pang to my distresses, as I feared he was already sent to Oung-pen-la.

If I ever felt the value and efficacy of prayer, I did at this time. I could not rise from my couch; I could make no efforts to secure my husband; I could only plead with that great and powerful Being who has said, 'Call upon me in the day of trouble, and *I will hear*, and thou shalt glorify me;' and who made me at this time feel so powerfully this promise, that I became quite composed, feeling assured that my prayers would be answered (314–15).

On hearing of Judson's plight the governor of the north gate offered himself as security for Judson, and agreed to keep Adoniram as a 'prisoner at large' in his own home; he could bring his family with him. The moment he could, first thing in the morning on 1 December 1825, Adoniram rushed to their old home, free at last to find Ann. She had been ill for a month with cerebral spinal meningitis. He later described the shock of their meeting to Emily, who captured the scene as follows:

With a step more fleet than for the last two years he had practised, and in spite of the maimed ankles, which sometimes almost refused their office, he hurried along the street to his beloved home. The door stood invitingly open, and, without having been seen by anyone, he entered. The first object which met his eye was a fat, half-naked Burman woman, squatting in the ashes beside a pan of coals, and holding on her knees a wan baby, so begrimed with dirt that it did not occur to the father it could be his own. He gave but one hasty look, and hurried to the next room. Across the foot of the bed, as though she had fallen there, lay a human object, that, at the first glance, was scarcely more recognisable than his child. The face was of a ghastly paleness, the features sharp, and the whole form shrunken almost to the last degree of emaciation. The glossy black curls had all been shorn from the finely-shaped head, which was now covered by a close-fitting cotton cap, of the coarsest and—unlike anything usually coming in contact with that head—not the cleanest kind. The whole room presented an appearance of the very extreme of wretchedness, more harrowing to the feelings that can be told. There lay the devoted wife, who had followed him so unweariedly from prison to prison, ever alleviating his distresses, without even common hireling attendance. He knew, by the very arrangement of the room, and by the expression of sheer animality on the face of the woman who held his child, that the Bengalee cook had been her only nurse. The wearied sleeper was awakened by a breath that came too near her cheek. Perhaps a falling tear might have been added; for steady as were those eyes in difficulties, dauntless in dangers, and stern when conscience frowned, they were well used to tender tears.[2]

When Ann could be moved, Adoniram took her to the governor's house. She began, slowly, to recover. But they were still not free to leave Ava, and there was no certainty regarding their future. The Burmese were oscillating between negotiation and military resistance. They were not going to release Adoniram voluntarily; he was an asset both for translation work and as a hostage.

Eventually, the British insisted on the release of the Judsons as one of the terms of peace, and they were able to leave Ava on 21 February 1826 for the British camp at Yantabo. Dr Price had chosen to stay in the employment of the Burmese king.[3] Ann described their departure:[4]

> ... we took an affectionate leave of the good-natured officer who had so long entertained us at his house, and who now accompanied us to the water side, and we then left for ever the banks of Ava.

> It was on a cool, moonlight evening ... that with hearts filled with gratitude to God, and overflowing with joy at our prospects, we passed down the Irrawaddy, surrounded by six or eight golden boats, accompanied by all we had on earth. The thought that we had still to pass the Burmese camp, would sometimes occur to damp our joy, for we feared that some obstacle might there arise to retard our progress. Nor were we mistaken in our conjectures. We reached the camp about midnight, where we were detained two hours ...

> Mr. Judson ... strenuously insisted that he would not remain, but go on immediately. The officers were finally prevailed on to consent, hoping much from Mr. Judson's assistance in making peace.

We now, for the first time, for more than a year and a half, felt that we were free, and no longer subject to the oppressive yoke of the Burmese. And with what sensations of delight, on the next morning, did I behold the masts of the steam boat, the sure presage of being within the bounds of civilized life! As soon as our boat reached the shore, Brigadier A. and another officer came on board, congratulated us on our arrival, and invited us on board the steam boat, where I passed the remainder of the day; while your brother went on to meet the general, who, with a detachment of the army, had encamped at Yandaboo, a few miles further down the river. Mr. Judson returned in the evening, with an invitation from Sir Archibald, to come immediately to his quarters, where I was the next morning introduced, and received with the greatest kindness by the general, who had a tent pitched for us near his own—took us to his own table, and treated us with the kindness of a father, rather than as strangers of another country.

We feel that our obligations to General Campbell can never be cancelled. Our final release from Ava, and our recovering all the property that had there been taken, was owing entirely to his efforts. His subsequent hospitality, and kind attention to the accommodations for our passage to Rangoon, have left an indelible impression on our minds, which can never be forgotten. We daily received the congratulations of the British officers, whose conduct towards us formed a striking contrast to that of the Burmese. I presume to say, that no persons on earth were ever happier, than we were during the fortnight we passed at the English camp. For several days, this single idea wholly occupied my mind, that we were out of the power of the Burmese government, and once more under the protection of the English. Our feelings

continually dictated expressions like these, *What shall we render unto the Lord, for all his benefits towards us?* (320–22).

On 24 February the treaty of peace was signed by the British and Burmese commissioners. General Campbell gave a great dinner party to mark the event, later recalled by Adoniram:

General Campbell was to give a dinner to the Burmese commissioners, and he chose to make it an affair of some pomp and magnificence. At a given order, almost as by magic, the camp was turned into a scene of festivity, with such a profusion of gold and crimson, and floating banners, as is thought most pleasing to an Oriental eye. When the dinner-hour arrived, the company marched in couples, to the music of the band, toward the table, led by the general, who walked alone. As they came opposite the tent with the veranda before it, suddenly the music ceased, the whole procession stood still, and while the wondering Burmans turned their eager eyes in every direction, doubtful as to what would be the next act in the little drama, so curious to them as strangers, the general entered the tent. In a moment he reappeared with a lady on his arm,—no stranger to the conscious commissioners,—whom he led to the table, and seated at his own right hand. The abashed commissioners slid into their seat shrinkingly, where they sat as though transfixed by a mixture of astonishment and fear. 'I fancy these gentleman must be old acquaintances of yours, Mrs. Judson,' General Campbell remarked, amused by what he began to suspect, though he did not fully understand it; 'and, judging from their appearance, you must have treated them very ill.' Mrs. Judson smiled. The Burmans could not understand the remark, but they evidently considered themselves the subject of it, and their faces were blank with consternation.

'What is the matter with yonder owner of the pointed beard?'
pursued Sir Archibald; 'he seems to be seized with an ague-fit.'

'I do not know,' answered Mrs. Judson, fixing her eyes on the
trembler, with perhaps a mischievous enjoyment of his anxiety,
'unless his memory may be too busy. He is an old acquaintance
of mine, and may probably infer danger to himself from seeing
me under your protection.'

She then proceeded to relate how, when her husband was
suffering from fever, in the stifled air of the inner prison, with
five pairs of fetters about his ankles, she had walked several miles
to this man's house to ask a favour. She had left home early in the
morning; but was kept waiting so long that it was noonday before
she proffered her request, and received a rough refusal. She was
turning sorrowfully away, when his attention was attracted by the
silk umbrella she carried in her hand, and he instantly seized upon
it. It was in vain that she represented the danger of her walking
home without it; told him she had brought no money, and could
not buy anything to shelter her from the sun; and begged that,
if he took that, he would at least furnish her with a paper one, to
protect her from the scorching heat. He laughed, and turning the
very suffering that had wasted her into a jest, told her it was only
stout people who were in danger of a sun-stroke—the sun could
not find such as she; and so turned her from the door.

Expressions of indignation burst from the lips of the listening
officers; and, try to restrain them as they would, indignant
glances did somewhat detract from that high tone of courtesy
which it is an Englishman's, and especially an English officer's,
pride to preserve in all matters of hospitality. The poor Burman,

conscience-taught, seemed to understand everything that was passing, and his features were distorted with fear; while his face, from which the perspiration oozed painfully, appeared, through his tawny skin, of a deathly paleness. It was not in a woman's heart to do other than pity him; and Mrs. Judson remarked softly, in Burmese, that he had nothing to fear, and then repeated the remark to Sir Archibald. The conversation immediately became general, and every means was taken to reassure the timorous guests, but with little success. There sat the lady, whom all but one of them had personally treated with indignity, at the right hand of power, and her husband, just released from his chains, close beyond; and they doubtless felt conscious that if they and their lady-wives were in such a position, they would ask the heads of their enemies, and the request would be granted.

'I never thought I was over and above vindictive,' remarked Mr. Judson, when he told the story; 'but really it was one of the richest scenes I ever beheld.'[5]

On 6 March 1826, Ann, Adoniram and baby Maria left the British camp. They were taken on the *Irrawaddy* gunboat down to Rangoon. A British officer, Lieutenant Calder Campbell, was attacked while sailing and taken on board the *Irrawaddy*. Ann dressed his wounds and took care of him. He later wrote:

We were taken on board. My eyes first rested on the thin, attenuated form of a lady—a white lady! the first white woman I had seen for more than a year! She was standing on the little deck of the row-boat, leaning on the arm of a sickly-looking gentleman with an intellectual cast of countenance, in whom I at once recognised the husband or the brother …

She was seated in a large sort of swinging chair, of American construction, in which her slight, emaciated, but graceful form appeared almost ethereal. Yet, with much of heaven, there were still the breathings of earthly feeling about her; for at her feet rested a babe,—a little, wan baby, on which her eyes often turned with all a mother's love; and gazing frequently upon her delicate features, with a fond yet fearful glance, was that meek missionary, her husband. Her face was pale, very pale, with that expression of deep and serious thought which speaks of the strong and vigorous mind within the frail and perishing body; her brown hair was braided over a placid and holy brow; but her hands—those small, lily hands—were quite beautiful; beautiful they were, and very wan; for ah! they told of disease—of death—death in all its transparent grace—when the sickly blood shines through the clear skin, even as the bright poison lights up the Venetian glass which it is about to shatter. That lady was Mrs. Judson, whose long captivity and severe hardships amongst the Burmese have since been detailed in her published journals.

I remained two days with them,—two delightful days they were to me. Mrs Judson's powers of conversation were of the first order, and the many affecting anecdotes that she gave us of their long and cruel bondage, their struggles in the cause of religion, and their adventures during a long residence at the court of Ava, gained a heightened interest from the beautiful, energetic simplicity of her language, as well as from the certainty I felt that so fragile a flower as she in very truth was, had but a brief season to linger on earth.[6]

Even making full allowance for the romantic tone of writing which was then quite acceptable, the reverence of this description illustrates

the way in which Ann was elevated to the status of a Protestant saint after her death.

The Judsons arrived in Rangoon on 21 March 1826, two years and three months after they had left for Ava with such high hopes. The scene there was grim. The mission house was in ruins; the church had been scattered. It looked as if their work there had been for nothing. Looking back over the past terrible months, they decided to draw a line and make a new start. Now there would be complete freedom to evangelize the area of Burma occupied by Britain, and they decided to focus their efforts in that area.

In July 1826 Ann finished the epic account she had been writing to her brother-in-law for the past two months. In the concluding pages she faced the painful question: why had she ignored such strong advice, and proceeded to Burma when war between Britain and Burma had been inevitable? Had not this stubborn insistence resulted in terrible and meaningless suffering? Ann was unwilling to admit culpability; she had followed her conscience:

A review of our trip to, and adventures in Ava, often excites the inquiry, Why were we permitted to go? What good has been effected? Why did I not listen to the advice of friends in Bengal, and remain there till the war was concluded? But all that we can say, is, *It is not in man that walketh, to direct his steps.* So far as my going round to Rangoon, at the time I did, was instrumental in bringing those heavy afflictions upon us, I can only state, that if I ever acted from a sense of duty in my life, it was at that time; for my conscience would not allow me any peace, when I thought of sending for your brother to come to Calcutta, in prospect of the approaching war. Our Society at home have lost no property in

consequence of our difficulties: but two years of precious time have been lost to the mission, unless some future advantage may be gained, in consequence of the severe discipline to which we ourselves have been subject. We are sometimes induced to think, that the lesson we found so very hard to learn, will have a beneficial effect through our lives; and that the mission may, in the end, be advanced rather than retarded.

We should have had no hesitation about remaining in Ava, if no part of the Burmese Empire had been ceded to the British. But as it was, we felt it would be an unnecessary exposure, besides the missionary field being much more limited, in consequence of intoleration. We now consider our future missionary prospects as bright indeed; and our only anxiety is, to be once more in that situation, where our time will be exclusively devoted to the instruction of the heathen ...

This letter, dreadful as are the scenes herein described, gives you but a faint idea of the awful reality. The anguish, the agony of mind, resulting from a thousand little circumstances impossible to delineate on paper, can be known by those only who have been in similar situations. Pray for us, my dear brother and sister, that these heavy afflictions may not be in vain, but may be blessed to our spiritual good, and the advancement of Christ's church among the heathen (322–3).

The cost of these years, however, was higher than Ann realized. Her health had been broken, and the mission was about to lose one of its most valuable resources.

22

'On earth we serve God—in heaven we praise him' (1826)

Overjoyed at their new freedom, Ann and Adoniram had high hopes for the future. Under the terms of the Treaty of Yandabo, the British annexed the two sizeable territories of Arakan and Tenasserim (see map on page 230). There would be ample scope for missionary work in these two territories, with religious toleration ensured. Just ten days after their arrival in Rangoon, Adoniram joined the British Civil Commissioner, Mr Crawfurd, on an exploratory trip to decide on a site for the British Headquarters in the southern territory of Tenasserim. Leaving Rangoon on 31 March 1826, they selected a site at the mouth of the River Salween. At a ceremony of dedication on 6 April it was named Amherst, and Adoniram was called on to give a reading and prayer. He returned to Rangoon on 10 April and began making preparation to move to Amherst. Four of the Burmese Christian families were sent on ahead. Ann wrote optimistically to Mrs Chaplin on 6 June 1826:

Map of Burma after the Anglo-Burman war of 1824–6

And yet I trust the prosperity of the Burman mission, (still the dearest object of our hearts) will be promoted by those events, which have taken place the last two years. We have no longer to solicit the patronage of a haughty monarch, for the establishment of our mission, or to court the favour of the Woongyees, to prevent the persecution of the converts; but in future shall be allowed to sit under our own vine and fig tree, and call to perishing immortal beings to listen to the glad tidings of the gospel.

We are now busily employed in preparing for our departure to Amherst. We shall doubtless be obliged to go through many trials, as it is a new place, and no houses yet built. But the Burmese population will be considerable, and we shall have every advantage for prosecuting the mission. Four of our Christian families have already gone, and we shall follow in a few days. My female school will, I trust, soon be in operation—then you shall hear from me constantly (324).

To another friend she wrote:

For nineteen months we were prisoners at Ava, suffering everything from oppression and poverty you can imagine. I am at times so amazed to find we still exist and are certainly out of the hand of tyranny, that it seems as though a miracle had been wrought to effect it. Twice in the midst of our sufferings I was reduced by sickness beyond all hope, but almost without human agency, restored again to health. Oh! How much we owe to that kind Being who has mingled mercy with all our afflictions. We are now preparing to remove to Amherst, a new town lately built by the English Government on part of that territory ceded by the Burman Government in the late treaty. It will be quite

full of Burmans, as whole families are now crowding thither to enjoy the protection of the British Government. Here if our lives are spared we intend establishing the Mission, and shall have as many schools under our direction as funds will allow. Most of the Christians go with us. Our faithful Moung Ing stood by us in all our afflictions at Ava, and we intend rewarding him by making him master of one of the schools, for which he is well qualified. Mah-men-lah is as firm as ever. She will also be employed in the schools. Let our favourite motto:- *'On earth we serve God—in heaven we praise Him'* ever stimulate us to constant and unwearied exertion to promote that blessed cause in which we are allowed to be engaged.[1]

A letter to her close friend Mrs Deakin written from Rangoon on 12 May gives a glimpse of her hopes for the future:

> Our little Maria is now fifteen months old, a lovely child with blue eyes and light hair. Her name is Maria Eliza Butterworth. *The next* shall be a Deakin. Pray for us, that we may be faithful unto death.[2]

The Judsons left Rangoon on 29 June and arrived at Amherst on 2 July. The superintendent of Amherst let them have the use of a house he had intended for himself, while they supervised the building of a suitable mission house. Adoniram made sure that Ann was settled and that plans were in order for the building. Then, just three days after their arrival, he had to leave her again.

He had no desire to do so. He left Amherst in order to accompany Mr Crawfurd in his negotiations with the Burmese government. Adoniram hated such negotiations. He wanted to get on with mission

work and to be with his family. However his greatest desire was to see the gospel established in Burma—not just the part occupied by the British, but the portion still controlled by the Burmese king. Crawfurd held out the possibility that they might be able to secure a measure of religious toleration in the Burmese empire. This incentive proved irresistible. Ann urged Adoniram to go. Adoniram described the settlement at Amherst and his decision to leave in a letter written from Rangoon on 31 July 1826:

Rev. and dear Sir,

At the date of my last letter, I was waiting for an opportunity of removing to Amherst. Since then, the Commissioner, Mr. Crawfurd, who is appointed to negotiate a secondary treaty with the court of Ava, renewed his proposal for me to accompany the embassy, and pledged himself, in case of my complying, to use his interest to procure the insertion of an article in the treaty, favourable to religious toleration,—an object which I have had at heart so many years, and which, though on account of the opening in the south provinces not so necessary as formerly, yet greatly favourable to the gradual introduction of religion, into all parts of the country, from the station which we propose occupying. With these views, I thought it my duty to accept the offer. Desirous, however, of making a commencement in the new place as early as possible, and unwilling to disappoint the native converts, who had left this, in the full expectation of our immediately following them, I accompanied Mrs. Judson and family thither, in the end of last month, and after seeing them comfortably settled, in a temporary house belonging to Capt. Fenwick, Civil Superintendent of the place, which he

kindly vacated for Mrs Judson's accommodation, I returned to Rangoon the 9th inst.

The new town has made some progress during the rains. About fifty native houses—Burmese; Chinese, and Indian Musselmen, and three or four Europeans, exclusive of barracks for the troops, and officers' houses, compose the infant settlement. As soon as the favourable season commences, it will increase rapidly, in consequence of large emigrations from Rangoon. Numerous villages are even now springing up, on the eastern side of the Salwen; and there can be no doubt, that the whole region will evidently be filled with a native population. The harbour of Amherst proves to be safe and commodious; large forests of teak wood have been discovered in the interior, thereby ensuring it a place of trade,—the situation of the settlement, exposed at all seasons to the sea breeze, must be healthy; and the mission, I may venture to say, will receive the decided patronage of government. The management of all the ceded provinces will probably be entrusted to Mr. Crawfurd, one of the most enlightened, intelligent, liberal men I have ever met—one most eminently qualified to discharge the highest and most responsible duties of government.

The embassy will leave this for Ava, on the receipt of final orders from Bengal, which are daily expected. I hope that the object of the embassy will be obtained in the course of three or four months; and that I shall be able to reach Amherst, and recommence missionary operations in November next (327–8).

Adoniram had left Amherst on 5 July 1826. This time it had not been too hard to say goodbye since the absence was expected to be

relatively short. But Adoniram and Crawfurd only arrived in Ava on 30 September, and it soon became clear that the Burmese government had absolutely no intention of granting religious liberty. Adoniram's presence at the negotiations was, as far as he was concerned, a waste of precious time. He had initially reckoned on being away for between four and five months; soon it became obvious that it would be seven or eight months before he would be able to return to Amherst.

And then, on 24 November, the crushing news arrived. Ann had died a month earlier, on 24 October, aged only thirty-seven.

Adoniram wrote from Ava to Ann's mother on 7 December 1826:

Dear mother,

This letter, though intended to the whole family, I address particularly to you; for it is a mother's heart that will be most deeply interested in its melancholy details. I propose to give, at different times, some account of my great irreparable loss, of which you will have heard before receiving this letter.

I left your daughter, my beloved wife, at Amherst, the 5th of July last, in good health, comfortably situated, happy in being out of the reach of our savage oppressors, and animated in prospect of a field of missionary labour opening under the auspices of British protection. It affords me some comfort, that she not only consented to my leaving her, for the purpose of joining the present embassy to Ava, but uniformly gave her advice in favour of the measure, whenever I hesitated concerning my duty. Accordingly, I left her. On the 5th of July, I saw her for the last time. Our parting was much less painful, than many others had been. We

had been preserved through so many trials and vicissitudes, that
a separation of three or four months, attended with no hazards
to either party, seemed a light thing. We parted, therefore, with
cheerful hearts, confident of a speedy reunion, and indulging
fond anticipations of future years of domestic happiness. After
my return to Rangoon, and subsequent arrival at Ava, I received
several letters from her, written in her usual style, and exhibiting
no subject of regret or apprehension, except the declining health
of our little daughter Maria. Her last was dated the 14th of Sept.
She says, 'I have this day moved into the new house, and for the
first time since we were broken up at Ava, feel myself at home.
The house is large and convenient, and if you were here, I should
feel quite happy. The native population is increasing very fast,
and things wear rather a favourable aspect. Moung Ing's school
has commenced with ten scholars, and more are expected. Poor
little Maria is still feeble. I sometimes hope she is getting better;
then again she declines to her former weakness. When I ask
her where Papa is, she always starts up and points towards the
sea. The servants behave very well, and I have no trouble about
any thing, excepting you and Maria. Pray take care of yourself,
particularly as it regards the intermittent fever at Ava. May God
preserve and bless you, and restore you in safety to your new and
old home, is the prayer of your affectionate Ann.'

On the 3d of Oct. Capt. F—, Civil Superintendant of Amherst,
writes, 'Mrs. Judson is extremely well.' Why she did not write
herself by the same opportunity, I know not. On the 18th, the
same gentleman writes, 'I can hardly think it right to tell you,
that Mrs. Judson has had an attack of fever, as before this reaches
you, she will, I sincerely trust, be quite well, as it has not been
so severe as to reduce her. This was occasioned by too close

attendance on the child. However, her cares have been rewarded in a most extraordinary manner, as the poor babe, at one time, was so reduced, that no rational hope could be entertained of its recovery; but at present a most favourable change has taken place, and she has improved wonderfully. Mrs. Judson had no fever last night, so that the intermission is now complete.' The tenor of this letter was such, as to make my mind quite easy, both as it regarded the mother and the child. My next communication was a letter with a black seal, handed me by a person, saying he was sorry to inform me of the death of the child. I know not whether this was a mistake on his part, or kindly intended to prepare my mind for the real intelligence. I went into my room, and opened the letter with feelings of gratitude and joy, that at any rate the mother was spared. It was from Mr. B—, Assistant Superintendant of Amherst, dated the 26th of Oct. and began thus:

'My dear Sir, to one who has suffered so much and with such exemplary fortitude, there needs but little preface to tell a tale of distress. It were cruel indeed to torture you with doubt and suspense. To sum up the unhappy tidings in a few words—*Mrs. Judson is no more.*'

At intervals, I got through with the dreadful letter, and proceed to give you the substance, as indelibly engraven on my heart.

'Early in the month she was attacked with a most violent fever. From the first she felt a strong presentiment that she could not recover, and on the 24th, about eight in the evening, she expired. Dr. R—was quite assiduous in his attentions, both as friend and physician. Capt. F—procured her the services of a European woman from the 45th regiment; and be assured all

was done, that could be done, to comfort her in her sufferings, and to smooth the passage to the grave. We all feel deeply the loss of this excellent lady, whose shortness of residence among us was yet sufficiently long, to impress us with a deep sense of her worth and virtues. It was not until about the 20th that Dr. R. began seriously to suspect danger. Before that period, the fever had abated at intervals; but its last approach baffled all medical skill. On the morning of the 23d, Mrs. Judson spoke for the last time. The disease had then completed its conquest, and from that time up to the moment of dissolution, she lay nearly motionless, and apparently quite insensible. Yesterday morning, I assisted in the last melancholy office of putting her mortal remains in the coffin; and in the evening her funeral was attended by all the European officers now resident here. We have buried her near the spot where she first landed; and I have put up a small rude fence around the grave to protect it from incautious intrusions.—Your little girl Maria is much better. Mrs. W—has taken charge of her; and I hope she will continue to thrive under her care.'...

I will not trouble you, my dear mother, with an account of my own private feelings—the bitter heart-rending anguish, which for some days would not admit of mitigation, and the comfort which the Gospel subsequently afforded, the Gospel of Jesus Christ, which brings life and immortality to light. Blessed assurance—and let us apply it afresh to our hearts—that while I am writing and you perusing these lines, her spirit is resting and rejoicing in the heavenly paradise (330–34).

Adoniram arrived back in Amherst on 24 January 1827. Six months earlier he had taken leave of his family with every hope that they would soon be reunited to make their new start together. The homecoming

was bitter. Even his little daughter did not recognize him and turned away from his embrace. He moved in with Jonathan and Deborah Wade, who had arrived in Amherst shortly after Ann's death and taken charge of Maria. The next task was to glean as much information as possible about Ann's last weeks and days. On 4 February 1827 he again wrote to Ann's mother with those details he had been able to obtain:

> Amid the desolation that death has made, I take up my pen once more to address the mother of my beloved Ann. I am sitting in the house she built—in the room where she breathed her last—and at a window from which I see the tree that stands at the head of her grave, and the top of the 'small rude fence' which they have put up 'to protect it from incautious intrusion.'

> Mr. and Mrs. Wade are living in the house, having arrived here about a month after Ann's death; and Mrs. Wade has taken charge of my poor motherless Maria. I was unable to get any accounts of the child at Rangoon: and it was only on my arriving here, the 24th ult. that I learned she was still alive. Mr. Wade met me at the landing place: and as I passed on to the house, one and another of the native Christians came out, and when they saw me, they began to weep. At length we reached the house; and I almost expected to see my love coming out to meet me, as usual; but no, I saw only in the arms of Mrs. Wade, a poor little puny child, who could not recognize her weeping father, and from whose infant mind had long been erased all recollections of the mother who loved her so much.

> She turned away from me in alarm, and I, obliged to seek comfort elsewhere, found my way to the grave; but who ever obtained comfort there? Thence I went to the house, in which

I left her; and looked at the spot where we last knelt in prayer, and where we exchanged the parting kiss.

The doctor who attended her, has removed to another station, and the only information I can obtain is such as the native Christians are able to communicate.

It seems that her head was much affected during her last days, and she said but little. She sometimes complained thus—The teacher is long in coming, and the new Missionaries are long in coming; I must die alone and leave my little one; but as it is the will of God, I acquiesce in his will. I am not afraid of death, but I am afraid I shall not be able to bear these pains. Tell the teacher that the disease was most violent, and I could not write; tell him how I suffered and died; tell him all that you see; and take care of the house and things until he returns. When she was unable to take notice of any thing else, she would still call the child to her and charge the nurse to be kind to it, and indulge it in every thing, until its father should return. The last day or two, she lay almost senseless and motionless, on one side—her head reclining on her arm—her eyes closed—and at 8 in the evening, with one exclamation of distress in the Burman language, she ceased to breathe …

The doctor is decidedly of opinion that the fatal termination of the fever is not to be ascribed to the localities of the new settlement, but chiefly to the weakness of her constitution, occasioned by severe privations and long protracted sufferings which she endured at Ava. Oh, with what meekness, patience, magnanimity, and Christian fortitude, she bore those sufferings! And can I wish they had been less? Can I sacrilegiously wish to

rob her crown of a single gem? Much she saw and suffered of the evil of this evil world; and eminently was she qualified to relish and enjoy the pure and holy rest into which she has entered. True, she has been taken from a sphere, in which she was singularly qualified, by her natural disposition, her winning manners, her devoted zeal, and her perfect acquaintance with the language, to be extensively serviceable to the cause of Christ; true, she has been torn from her husband's bleeding heart, and from her darling babe; but infinite wisdom and love have presided, as ever, in this most afflicting dispensation. Faith decides, that it is all right, and the decision of faith, eternity will soon confirm (335–7).

23

Epilogue

Adoniram was broken with grief. He had only little Maria as a link with the one he had loved ever since he set eyes on her that day back in Bradford so many years before. And Maria was so fragile. There were continual alarms regarding her health. On 24 April 1827, six months after her mother died, the baby succumbed to a fever, aged two years and three months. Her health had probably been shattered, as her mother's had been, during those terrible months at Oung-pen-la. Once again, Adoniram had to convey the news to Ann's mother. He wrote from Amherst on 26 April 1827:

Dear Mother Hasseltine,

My sweet little Maria lies by the side of her fond mother. The complaint, to which she was subject several months, [an affliction of the bowels] proved incurable. She had the best medical advice; and the kind care of Mrs. Wade could not have been in any respect exceeded by that of her own mother. But all our efforts,

and prayers, and tears, could not propitiate the cruel disease. The work of death went forward; and after the usual process, excruciating to a parent's feelings, she ceased to breathe, on the 24th inst. at three o'clock p.m. aged two years and three months. We then closed her faded eyes, and bound up her discoloured lips, where the dark touch of death first appeared, and folded her little hands—the exact pattern of her mother's, on her cold breast. The next morning, we made her last bed, in the small inclosure which surrounds her mother's lonely grave. Together they rest in hope, and under the hope tree, [Hopia] which stands at the head of the graves: and together, I trust, their spirits are rejoicing, after a short separation of precisely six months.

Thus I am left alone in the wide world. My father's family, and all my relatives, have been, for many years, separated from me, by seas that I shall never repass. They are the same to me as if buried. My own dear family I have actually buried: one in Rangoon, and two in Amherst. What remains for me, but to hold myself in readiness to follow the dear departed to that blessed world …? (338)

A week before Maria's death, two new missionaries arrived at Amherst. George and Sarah Boardman, with the Wades, rallied round to comfort Adoniram. But he seemed inconsolable. With iron discipline he continued to work. He continued writing, translating and preaching. He oversaw the removal of the mission from Amherst, which proved not to be viable as the British capital, to Moulmain, the preferred new location. As the mission in Burma expanded, he was undoubtedly the leader and driving force. But something seemed to have died inside him. The terrible privations of the war years, and then the appalling loss of his wife and daughter, left him with huge and unanswered questions.

He entered a 'dark night of the soul' experience, during which a literal lengthy sojourn by an open grave in the jungle symbolized something of the further death to self he was undergoing. During this time he searched out every possible area in which he might be proud—and crucified it. In May 1828 he renounced the title of Doctor of Divinity, conferred on him by Brown University in 1823. The same month he handed over all his personal financial resources to the mission board. He ordered the destruction of all his letters home. On 24 October 1828, the second anniversary of Ann's death, he moved into a solitary retreat which he called the Hermitage.

However, Adoniram did come through the crisis. He would never forget Ann, Roger and Maria, but time did heal. And even in the depths of his grief he had clung onto the certain hope of the resurrection of the dead. He wrote to Ann's sisters on 4 December 1827:

> Death mocks at us, and tramples our dearest hopes and our lives in the dust. Dreadful tyrant, offspring and ally of sin! But go on now, and do thy worst. Thy time will come. The last enemy that shall be destroyed, is death. Yes, awful power, thou shalt devour thyself and die. And then my angelic Ann, and my meek blue-eyed Roger, and my tender hearted, affectionate, darling Maria,—my venerable father, you, my dear sisters, that still remain, our still surviving parents, and I hope, myself, though all unworthy, shall be rescued from the power of death and the grave; and when the crown of life is set on our heads, and we know assuredly that we shall die no more, we shall make heaven's arches ring with songs of praise to Him, who hath loved us and washed us from our sins in his own blood …

> How happy should I be to find myself once more in the bosom of the family in Bradford, and tell you ten thousand things I

cannot put on paper. But this will never be. Nor is it of much consequence. A few more rolling suns, and you will hear of my death, or I of yours. Till then, believe me your most affectionate brother. And when we meet in heaven—when all have arrived, and we find all safe, for ever safe, and our Saviour ever safe and glorious, and in him, all his beloved—oh shall we not be happy, and ever praise Him who has endured the cross to wear and confer such a crown! (339–41).

Bereavement enabled Adoniram to identify closely with the feelings of those who suffered. Five years after Ann's death, his young colleague George Boardman died, leaving Sarah a widow aged twenty-seven. Adoniram immediately wrote a letter which came right from the heart:

My dear Sister:

You are now drinking the bitter cup whose dregs I am somewhat acquainted with. And though, for some time, you have been aware of its approach, I venture to say that it is far bitterer than you expected. It is common for persons in your situation to refuse all consolation, to cling to the dead, and to fear that they shall too soon forget the dear object of their affections. But don't be concerned. I can assure you that months and months of heartrending anguish are before you, whether you will or not. I can only advise you to take the cup with both hands, and sit down quietly to the bitter repast which God has appointed for your sanctification. As to your beloved, you *know* that all his tears are wiped away, and that the diadem which encircles his brow outshines the sun. Little Sarah and the other have again found their father, not the frail, sinful mortal that they left on earth, but an immortal saint, a magnificent, majestic king. What

more can you desire for them? While, therefore, your tears flow, let a due proportion be tears of joy. Yet take the bitter cup with both hands, and sit down to your repast. You will soon learn a secret, that there is sweetness at the bottom. You will find it the sweetest cup that you ever tasted in all your life. You will find heaven coming near to you, and familiarity with your husband's voice will be a connecting link, drawing you almost within the sphere of celestial music.[1]

Three years later Adoniram and Sarah married. And after Sarah's death, Adoniram would marry again. But there was always the certainty that Ann, and then Sarah, had gone before to glory, and that one day there would be a reunion more glorious than could ever be imagined. As he wrote to Emily:

Heaven will be brighter to me for thy presence. Thou wilt be with Ann and Sarah. We shall all join in the same song of love and praise; and how happy shall we be in beholding each other's faces glow with heavenly rapture, as we drink in the life-giving, joy-inspiriting smiles of Him whom we shall love above all![2]

Or, even more eloquently, in this letter Adoniram wrote to Emily we catch the vision of the eternal reward for which Ann laboured:

I seem to have lived in several worlds; but you are the earthly sun that illuminates my present. My thoughts and affections revolve around you, and cling to your form, and face, and lips. Other luminaries have been extinguished in death. I think of them with mournful delight, and anticipate the time when we shall all shine together as the brightness of the firmament and as the stars for ever and ever.[3]

Appendix I: Ann's legacy

What had Ann's life achieved?

First of all, she and her husband Adoniram had been used to pioneer a church-planting work in Burma. They had not been the first missionaries there; the prayers and labours of Felix Carey and others had gone before. But they were the first missionaries to stay there! All previous missionaries had either left, or entered government service. They also had the privilege of seeing the first Burmese people converted and of establishing the first church. From the start Ann had felt the same missionary 'call' as her husband, and worked alongside him as a 'co-labourer'. She was fully engaged in teaching and personal work in the *zayat* and she engaged in translation work in both Burmese and Siamese. The catechism she translated became a vital tool in instructing young converts. None of Ann's own children lived beyond the toddler stage, but many of the Burmese converts regarded her as their spiritual mother.

Secondly, humanly speaking, it was only because of her tireless efforts during the war that Adoniram's life was preserved. He not only

survived, but was subsequently able to work in Burma for a further twenty-three years, during which time a firm foundation for church life was laid in Burma. Patrick Johnstone, the author of *Operation World*, observes that the missionary zeal of the Baptist Church in Burma today still reflects something of the spirit of the Judsons.

Thirdly, Ann's writings were among the first to stir up missionary interest at a popular level among the Protestant population of both America and the United Kingdom. Her *Account of the American Baptist Mission to the Burman Empire* was widely read. She also provided spirited contributions for missionary magazines, which aimed to produce a reaction on the part of her readers. For example, she wrote the following lines for the *Missionary Magazine* of 1818:

> Let those who plead the native innocence and purity of heathen nations visit Burmah! The system of religion here has no power over the heart or restraint on the passions. Though it forbids, on pain of many years' suffering in hell, theft and falsehood, yet, I presume to say, there is not a single Burman in the country, who, if he had a good opportunity, without danger of detection, would hesitate to do either. Though the religion inculcates benevolence, tenderness, forgiveness of injuries, and love of enemies—though it forbids sensuality, love of pleasure, and attachment to worldly objects—yet it is destitute of power to produce the former, or to subdue the latter, in its votaries. In short, the Burman system of religion is like an alabaster image, perfect and beautiful in all it parts, but destitute of life. Besides being destitute of life, it provides no atonement for sin. Here also the Gospel triumphs over this and every other religion in the world.[1]

Fourthly, she was a passionate advocate of female education. All proceeds from her *Account* were to be ploughed back into schools for girls in Burma. On her first arrival in India she had been tremendously impressed with the girls' school at Serampore run by Hannah Marshman. She wrote home at that time:

> Good female schools are extremely needed in this country. I hope no Missionary will ever come out here, without a wife, as she, in her sphere, can be equally useful with her husband. I presume Mrs. Marshman does more good in her school, than half the ministers in America (75).

This subject was treated at greater length in Ann's *Address to Females in America, Relative to the Situation of Heathen Females in the East,* written in 1822 (see Appendix II).

At the time of her death, Ann had already started a girls' school in Amherst. The next year Adoniram wrote that there were fifteen girls in the 'Native Female Boarding School' and that Mrs Wade taught them for seven and a half hours a day (362). The school moved to Moulmain in November 1827.

Mrs Wade continued to take in little girls from backgrounds of terrible poverty and suffering, including some slaves. Her description of one little girl is included to give some indication of why Ann had felt so passionately the need for money to redeem slaves. The child was a slave of seven years old, and some residents of Moulmain told the missionaries she was likely to die because of vicious treatment from her master. Adoniram went to the owner and threatened that if he did not hand the girl over to the mission he would be reported to the English magistrate. Mrs Wade wrote:

Her little body was wasted to a skeleton, and covered from head to foot with the marks of a large rattan, and blows from some sharp-edged thing which left a deep scar. Her forehead, one of her ears, and a finger, were still suffering from his blows, and did not heal for some time. Her master in a rage one day caught her by the arm, and gave it such a twist as to break the bone … Besides, she had a large and very dreadful burn upon her body, recently inflicted. Of this last horrid deed, delicacy forbids my attempting any description.

… after nursing her with unremitted care by night and day myself, for two weeks, I had the inexpressible satisfaction of seeing her begin to play with the little girls … (381–2)

Thus those who had responded to Ann's appeal to sponsor female orphans and redeemed slaves were assured that this work was continuing.

Fifthly, her life and death became an inspiration to a whole generation of American Christians. The *Memoir* was printed in 1829 and ran through many editions. There is no way of telling how many people it influenced. For example, Ann was the childhood heroine of both Adoniram's second and third wives. In 1815 a ten-year-old American girl, Sarah Hall, wept when she heard of the death of Ann's baby Roger, and she wrote a poem to mark the sad event. Little did she know that eighteen years later she would become the second Mrs Judson. And in 1828 a twelve-year-old factory girl, Emily Chubbuck, was similarly moved by Maria's death. Emily later wrote:

One day I took up a little, dingy, coarse newspaper … and my eye fell on the words, 'Little Maria lies by the side of her mother.'

I had read about the missionaries ... I knew therefore at once that the letter was from Mr Judson and that his little daughter was dead. How I pitied his loneliness!'[2]

Eighteen years later she was to become the third Mrs Judson. Emily said to a friend before ever meeting Judson, 'I have felt, ever since I read the *Memoir of Mrs Ann H. Judson* when I was a small child, that I must become a missionary.'[3]

In some ways indeed Ann seems superhuman. Her courage in leaving America, her dedication in insisting that her beloved husband remain with the young believers while she had to seek medical help abroad, above all her loyalty during the imprisonment of Adoniram and her disregard of risk to herself in her efforts on his behalf, inspire our admiration. The Lord undoubtedly gave Ann unusual gifts in terms of linguistic ability, determination and bravery, as well as spiritual gifts of zeal for souls, patience in working with enquirers and faith during times of desperate hardship. And yet she was only too human in that she suffered as intensely as any of us would suffer; she was not hard or insensitive or cold It was her passionate devotion to her husband that enabled her to persevere on his behalf during his imprisonment, but the depth of her love for him meant that witnessing him in such degrading and sordid circumstances was daily torture for her. During her illness when she was unable to nurse her baby, she was far more in agony for the plight of her hungry infant than mindful of her own pain. She was a woman who loved intensely; loved her husband, loved her children, loved the people of Burma, but above all loved her God.

Appendix II: Address to Females in America, Relative to the Situation of Heathen Females in the East[1]

In the land of my birth, rendered doubly dear from the long entertained thought of never again beholding it; in the country favoured by Heaven above most others; it is with no common sensations I address my sisters and female friends on this most interesting subject. Favoured as we are from infancy with instruction of every kind, used as we are to view the female mind in its proper state, and accustomed as we are to feel the happy effects of female influence, our thoughts would fain turn away from the melancholy subject of female degradation, of female wretchedness. But will our feelings of pity and compassion, will those feelings which alone render the female character lovely, allow us to turn away—to dismiss the subject altogether, without making an effort to rescue—to save? No! I think I hear your united voices echo the reply: 'Our efforts shall be joined with yours. Show us the situation of our tawny sisters the other side of the world, and though the disgusting picture break our hearts, it will fill us with gratitude

to Him who has made us to differ, and excite to stronger exertion in their behalf.' Listen, then, to my tale of woe!

In Bengal and Hindostan, the females, in the higher classes, are excluded from the society of men. At the age of two or three years, they are married by their parents to children of their own rank in society. On these occasions all the parade and splendour possible are exhibited; they are then conducted to their father's abode, not to be educated, not to prepare for the performance of duties incumbent on wives and mothers, but to drag out the usual period allotted in listless idleness, in mental torpor. At the age of thirteen, fourteen, or fifteen, they are demanded by their husbands, to whose home they are removed, where again confinement is their lot. No social intercourse is allowed to cheer their gloomy hours; nor have they the consolation of feeling that they are viewed, even by their husbands, in the light of companions. So far from receiving those delicate attentions which render happy the conjugal state, and which distinguish civilized from heathen nations, the wife receives the appellation of *my servant,* or *my dog,* and is allowed to partake of what her lordly husband is pleased to give at the *conclusion* of his repast! In this secluded, degraded situation, females in India receive no instruction, consequently they are wholly uninformed of an eternal state. No wonder mothers consider female existence a curse; hence their desire to destroy their female offspring, and to burn themselves with the bodies of their deceased husbands. This last circumstance might imply some attachment, were it not a well known fact, that the *disgrace* of a woman who refuses to burn with the corpse of her husband is such, that her nearest relations would refuse her a morsel of rice to prevent her starvation. Thus, destitute of all enjoyment, both here and hereafter, are the females in Bengal. Such is their life, such is their death—and here the scene is closed to mortal view! But, they are amiable, say some, and destitute of those

violent passions which are exhibited among females in our own country. My beloved friends, be not deceived. Who ever heard that ignorance was favourable to the culture of amiable feelings? Their minds are in such a state of imbecility, that we might hope to find at least an absence of vicious feelings. But facts prove the contrary.—Whenever an opportunity for exhibiting the malignant passions of the soul occurs, human nature never made a more vigorous effort to discover her odious deformity, than has been observed in these secluded females.

But let us turn our eyes from the present picture, to one not less heart-rending, but where hope may have a greater influence to brighten and to cheer. The females in the Burman Empire, (containing a population far above the United States of America,) are not like the females in Bengal, secluded from all society. In this respect they are on an equality with ourselves. Wives are allowed the privilege of eating with heir husbands. They engage in domestic concerns, and thus, in some respects, the Burman females deserve our particular sympathy and attention. But they enjoy little of the confidence or affection of their husbands, and to be born a female is universally considered a peculiar misfortune. The wife and grown daughters are considered by the husband and father as much the subjects of discipline, as younger children; hence it is no uncommon thing for females of every age and description, to suffer under the tyrannic rod of those who should be their protectors.

Burmah, also, like her sister nations, suffers the female mind to remain in its native state, without an effort to show how much more highly she has been favoured. The females of this country are lively, inquisitive, strong and energetic, susceptible of friendship and the warmest attachment, and possess minds naturally capable of rising to the highest state of cultivation and refinement. But, alas! they are

taught nothing that has a tendency to cherish these best native feelings of the heart! That they possess strong energetic minds, is evident from their mode of conversing, and from that inquisitive turn which is so conspicuous. It may not, perhaps, be uninteresting to mention a particular display of mental energy as exhibited in the early inquiries of Mah Men-la.

Some time previous to our arrival in Rangoon, her active mind was led to inquire the origin of all things. If a Boodh was deity, who created all that her eyes beheld? She inquired of this person and that, visited all the teachers within the circle of her acquaintance, but none were able to give her satisfactory information on the subject. Her anxiety increased to such a degree, that her own family feared she would be deranged. She finally resolved on learning to read, that she might be able to gain the desired information from their sacred books. Her husband, willing to gratify her curiosity in this respect, taught her to read himself. After having acquired what very few Burman females are allowed to acquire, she studied the sacred books, which left her mind in the same inquisitive state as when she commenced. For ten years she had continued her inquiries, when, one day, a neighbour brought in a tract written by Mr. Judson, from which she derived her first ideas of an eternal God. Her next difficulty arose from her being ignorant of the residence of the author of the tract, and it was not till after the erection of the zayat, that this difficulty was removed. By her enquiries respecting the Christian religion, she evinced a mind, which, had it been early and properly cultivated, would have hardly been surpassed by females in our own country. And happy am I to add, that she not only became rationally and speculatively convinced of the truths of the Gospel, but was, I trust, taught to feel their power on her heart, by the influence of the Holy Spirit, embraced them, has become an

ornament to her profession, and her daily walk and conversation would shame many professors of religion in Christian countries.

Shall we, my beloved friends, suffer minds like these to lie dormant, to wither in ignorance and delusion, to grope their way to eternal ruin, without an effort on our part, to raise, to refine, to elevate, and to point to that Saviour who has died equally for them as for us? Shall we sit down in indolence and ease, indulge in all the luxuries with which we are surrounded, and which our country so bountifully affords, and leave beings like these, flesh and blood, intellect and feeling, like ourselves, and of *our own sex*, to perish, to sink into eternal misery? No! by all the tender feelings of which the female mind is susceptible, by all the privileges and blessings resulting from the cultivation and expansion of the human mind, by our duty to God and our fellow creatures, and by the blood and groans of Him who died on Calvary, let us make a united effort; let us call on all, old and young, in the circle of our acquaintance, to join us in attempting to meliorate the situation, to instruct, to enlighten and save females in the Eastern world; and though time and circumstances should prove that our united exertions have been ineffectual, we shall escape at death that bitter thought, that Burman females have been lost, without an effort of ours to prevent their ruin.

Ann H. Judson

Appendix III: Biographical Sketch of Adoniram Judson (1788–1850)

Adoniram never wrote a full autobiography. During a period of deep depression after the death of Ann, he ordered that all his private papers and letters be destroyed. Many records had in any case been burned by Ann during the ordeal in Ava during the Anglo-Burman War, and others were consumed in a house fire in Moulmain in 1847. But Adoniram did prepare a seven-page 'Autobiographical Record of Dates and Events' before he died, which was included as an appendix in the biography compiled by his son published in 1883. The facts in the following account are taken from this source.

Early years (1788–1808)

Adoniram Judson senior was vastly ambitious for his first-born son. He was himself a Congregational minister, but he cherished high hopes that his eldest son would achieve great status. The character of the younger Adoniram was indelibly affected by his father's aspirations. Burning ambition and total determination were to characterize his life. Ultimately these characteristics were to be focused on the evangelization of Burma.

Born in Malden, Massachusetts, on 9 August 1788, Adoniram junior certainly exhibited those natural gifts which fuelled his father's ambitions. A brilliant youngster, he excelled in everything he did. He also rebelled against his parents' faith. At the age of sixteen he was sent, a year early, to Providence College (later called Brown University). Here he was captivated by the daring of those students who professed to be free-thinkers and atheists. One of the leaders among these students was a powerful personality called Jacob Eames, who scoffed at everything that Adoniram had been brought up to value.

Adoniram graduated in 1807, having achieved the highest place in his year. Aged nineteen, he returned home to teach school. During his first year of teaching he had two textbooks published, one on grammar and the other on arithmetic. Life at home seemed very boring, and he soon left, to seek a more exciting life away from parental restraint.

Conversion (1808)

And then a remarkable 'coincidence' led to a spiritual revolution. One night, when Adoniram arrived at an inn, the only room left was next to that of a critically ill man. Throughout the night Adoniram was aware of the dying man's groans. In the morning he was devastated to learn that the dead man was his admired college mentor, Jacob Eames. Suddenly the daring of 'free thought' seemed pathetic. For where was Eames now? There was enough of Adoniram's upbringing left in him for him to be certain that after death comes judgement. He regarded this event as the voice of God; it was the beginning of the road back to faith.

Adoniram entered the Theological Institution at Andover, Massachusetts, in October 1808 and was converted the very next month. He became a member of the Third Congregational Church

in Plymouth in May 1809. In June he was offered, but declined, a post as tutor at Brown University; already he was crucifying his natural ambition. Then a book changed his life. When in September 1809 he obtained a copy of *Star in the East* by Buchanan, he was shaken to consider that at that time, apart from missions to the North American Indians, the American church had not sent out any foreign missionaries. And yet the majority of the world's population was perishing! How could American Christians 'sleep the sleep of death'? Several other young men at the seminary in Andover were thinking exactly the same way. A group of them covenanted together to serve overseas 'for life'.

The first American missionaries leave for Asia (1812)

On 28 June 1810 four young men, Judson, Nott, Newell and Mills, submitted a proposal to the General Association of Congregational Ministers, which would lead to the formation of America's first Protestant overseas mission agency (the American Board of Commissioners for Foreign Mission). Judson records that exactly a month later, on 28 July, he 'commenced an acquaintance with Ann Hasseltine'. He graduated with an M.A. from Brown University in September, and in January 1811 he was sent to England for consultation with the London Missionary Society. Back in America, the American Board of Commissioners appointed Judson, Nott, Newell and Hall as their first missionaries on 19 September 1811; they would soon be joined by a fifth, Luther Rice. The missionaries sailed for the East in February 1812. By now Judson, Newell and Nott had married, so they were accompanied by their wives.

The Judsons are baptized (6 September 1812)

On 1 September 1812, having arrived in India, Judson announced to the Secretary of the Board his change of views on baptism. He and Ann were baptized by immersion in Calcutta on 6 September 1812,

followed on 1st November by Luther Rice. The three of them could no longer, in all honesty, receive support from the body which had sent them out. They resigned from the Congregational Church, and sent letters back to the American Baptists, offering themselves as Baptist missionaries. In view of the appalling slowness of communications they knew that it would be years rather than months before they heard whether they had any support or not. Due to ill-health, Rice returned to America in March 1813. He proved to be a brilliant advocate of mission amongst the Baptists. The American Baptists did indeed accept the Judsons as their first overseas missionaries. Newell, Nott and Mills, still Congregationalists, continued for the moment in India. Within the next six years, each of them had either died or had to return to America because of ill-health.

Arrival in Burma (13 July 1813)
After many alarms and delays, the Judsons finally arrived in Rangoon, Burma, on 13 July 1813. The prospects seemed bleak. The government of Burma was a despotic tyranny, and the subjects of the Burmese king were not allowed to convert from Buddhism to other religions. The British Baptists had begun a mission in Burma, but the work had been hard and slow. Felix Carey (son of William Carey) and others had begun some work on translation, but by 1812 all missionaries apart from Felix had left. There had been no conversions; thus far there was no church. The year after the Judsons' arrival, Mrs Carey and the children drowned on the way up to Ava, and Felix Carey resigned from mission work.

Five years later Adoniram baptized the first convert. By August 1822, nine years after their arrival, eighteen Burmese converts had been baptized. By that time he had completed the translation of the New Testament into Burmese, together with a summary of the Old.

Imprisonment (8 June 1824–21 February 1826)

All mission work was suspended when war broke out between the English and the Burmese in 1824. The cause of the war was a series of disputes over British-controlled territory in north India. The effect was that the few foreigners in Burma were all equally suspect as spies and traitors and were thrown into prison, there to suffer conditions of medieval brutality. The British took control of Rangoon in May 1824, and the two missionary families there were able to leave for British-controlled India. But by this time the Judsons and Dr Jonathan Price had moved to the capital Ava. Adoniram and Jonathan were imprisoned, with all other foreigners, for the duration of the war. Ann remained free, and made every effort possible to mitigate the harshness of their conditions.

Ann's death (24 October 1826)

One of the terms of peace in February 1826 was that foreign prisoners should be free to leave for British-controlled territory if they so wished. Price decided to remain in Burmese government service. The Judsons resolved to continue with the mission in the part of the country controlled now by Britain. The site chosen for the British base in the southern area of the county was named Amherst. Here Ann, Adoniram and the remaining converts from Rangoon set up a new mission, and here Ann died in October 1826. Her health had been shattered by the privations suffered during the war. Her only surviving child, Maria, died exactly six months later. Adoniram was devastated. He had suffered so much during the war that he had few emotional reserves left. He continued working, even as he struggled through a black tunnel of depression and grief. He laboured for years on translating, then revising, the Bible in Burmese, and compiling a grammar and a dictionary. He was a perfectionist, and insisted on working from the original languages using the most up-to-date aids and tools available.

A new mission at Moulmain (1827)

Adoniram also supervised the transfer of the mission from Amherst. It had become obvious that the site at Amherst was not so suited as a British base as it had first seemed. The British army transferred their headquarters to Moulmain, and large numbers of people of various nationalities were moving there. Many Burmese nationals chose to live under British rather than Burmese rule, and the town grew rapidly. It was clear that this would be a far more strategic place than Amherst for the mission to be based. The Burmese converts, two couples from America (the Boardmans and the Wades) and Adoniram moved from Amherst to Moulmain during 1827.

Adoniram had to leave the graves of Ann and Maria at Amherst. He continued to grieve bitterly during the early years at Moulmain, going further and further in self-renunciation and withdrawing almost totally from any form of social life or recreation. But his iron determination ensured that work continued. In 1829 he wrote *The Golden Balance*, a tract in Burmese which proved enormously helpful in communicating with Buddhists. By now Judson was able to think along the lines of the Burmese, and communicate with concepts and ideas that were appropriate and comprehensible to them. He also completed his revision of his translation of the New Testament and the summary of the Old Testament. The next year, 1830, he attempted a mission back into the territory still controlled by the Burmese king, moving to Prome, a town beyond Rangoon. Here he continued translation, but also attempted evangelization among the local people. In 1831 he returned to Moulmain.

The translation of the Bible completed (31 January 1834)

Twenty-one years after his first arrival in Rangoon, Judson completed the translation of the whole Bible. He had arrived in Burma in July

1813, and he completed his translation on 31 January 1834. He then spent six years revising his work. The revised edition was published in 1840.

He did not work alone. To begin with, there had been the pioneer language work and translation accomplished by the British missionaries, Chater and Carey.[1] Then Judson was helped for years by Moung (Ko) En, a Burmese convert, and he used many other Burmese assistants. Adoniram read widely in Burmese literature to furnish his mind as fully as possible with every nuance of the idiom of the language and thought. As soon as missionary colleagues were competent in the language he would call on them to correct the translation, and he carefully weighed every suggestion. Wayland wrote:

> The importance of his work to millions of immortal souls was ever present to his view. He had been called by the providence of God to unfold to a whole nation, in their own language the revelation of the most High. He considered it to be a momentous undertaking; and a heavy weight would have rested on his soul if a single idea in the Scriptures had been rendered obscurely in consequence of haste, impatience, negligence, or culpable ignorance on the part of the translator.[2]

A distinguished linguist in India judged:

> We honour Wycliffe and Luther for their labours in their respective tongues, but what meed of praise is due to Judson for a translation of the Bible, *perfect as a literary work*, in a language so foreign to him as the Burmese?[3]

Evangelism

It is an irony that the greater part of Adoniram's time was spent labouring in the study when the great love of his life was preaching. He was increasingly frustrated by a chronic lung complaint, whereby any exertion of his voice led to dangerous spitting of blood. Whenever opportunity arose due to a break in the translation work, and when his health allowed, Adoniram revelled in village evangelism. But one of his cherished convictions was that indigenous workers were ultimately far more effective than foreign missionaries, and he had the joy of training and using many native preachers and evangelists. The freedom to evangelize offered by British protection was exploited to the full.

The native Burmese were, in the main, Buddhist, with a mind-set powerfully fixed against the notion of an eternal God. There was a huge amount of intellectual groundwork to be done; Adoniram and Ann had spent hundreds of hours in detailed discussion with enquirers, patiently chipping away at the many preconceptions which inhibited their understanding of the Christian message.

The Boardmans and the Karen people (1828–1834)

During the years following the war, the minority group of Karen people began to be reached. In March 1828 George and Sarah Boardman moved from Moulmain to Tavoy, the area inhabited by the Karen people. The Karen did not have centuries of Buddhist education and culture behind them. Their mind-set was far more amenable to accepting the Christian gospel. The Boardmans proved to be tireless in village evangelism among the Karen, walking for miles in rough hill terrain. The premature death of George Boardman in 1831 through tuberculosis was a terrible blow to the mission. Judson baptized the hundredth Karen convert in September 1833. Later hundreds more,

then thousands, were converted, churches planted and native workers appointed.

Marriage to Sarah Boardman (10 April 1834–1 September 1845)

George Boardman's young widow Sarah resisted all invitations to return to America. She was fluent in Burmese and Karen, and for three years she continued running a school, as well as engaging in evangelistic work. Adoniram had been deeply attached to both George and Sarah. They had helped him bury little Maria, and had comforted him after her death. Over the years Adoniram's respect for their dedication and abilities had grown. Having completed the translation of the whole Bible in January 1834, it is as if Adoniram now felt he could begin a new life. On 1st April he left for Tavoy to see Sarah Boardman, and they were married on 10 April. Three years had passed since George's death, eight years since that of Ann. Adoniram and Sarah found great happiness together.

Sarah was, like Ann, a tireless co-worker. Once settled in Moulmain with Adoniram, having already mastered the Burmese and Karen languages, she set out to learn the Taling dialect. There were many Taling (Peguan) people in Moulmain, and thus far none of the missionaries had been able to minister to them in their own language. Sarah soon began, with the help of a Peguin Christian, to translate tracts and a catechism. She also led prayer meetings and Bible classes.

In addition she gave Adoniram the family life he had never been able to enjoy with Ann. Children were born in October 1835, April 1837, July 1838, December 1839, March 1841 (this child was still born), July 1842, December 1843 and December 1844. While these little ones brought immense joy, there was also the ever-present spectre of

tropical sickness. Adoniram, Sarah and the children all succumbed to serious illness. In 1841 the family travelled to Serampore to try to find respite, but there little Henry died, aged one year and seven months. It seemed that others of the children might die also.

Eventually, like Ann before her, Sarah was told that she would die unless she returned to America. Since she was too weak to travel alone, Adoniram and the three older children sailed with her on 26 April 1845. The three younger ones were left in Burma.[4] Sarah deteriorated rapidly. They arrived on the island of St Helena on 26 August, and she died on 1 September 1845.

Return to America (1845–6)
Adoniram arrived back in America on 15 October, exhausted, bereaved and with the anxiety of having to find a home for Abby Ann, aged ten, Adoniram eight and Elnathan seven. Many conflicting emotions must have been evoked by this return to the homeland he had left thirty-three years before. Of his own family, only his sister Abigail was left. His parents and brother were dead. America itself was transformed: the frontier had shifted westwards and industrialization was leading to the creation of cities. The issue of slavery was dividing the states, as it was dividing the churches.

Adoniram and the others had left as mere youths, applauded by some, mocked by many. Now he arrived back to find himself a celebrity. The drama of the war years in Ava, the subsequent deaths of Ann and Maria, the tragic death of George Boardman, the heroic endeavours of his widow Sarah, the happy remarriage of Adoniram to Sarah and finally Sarah's premature death had been as near as the American public could wish to get to a soap opera—but all the better for being true, and so edifying! Adoniram was public property, and he hated

it. Invitations to preach flooded in, but before he left Burma he had
written to the Board pleading that he should not be booked up:
'Since there are thousands of preachers in English, and only five or
six Burmese preachers in the whole world, I may be allowed to hoard
up the remnant of my breath and lungs for the country where they
are most needed.'[5] His priorities were to get the children settled, find
someone to write a suitable memoir of Sarah and ensure continuing
support for the Burman mission. The latter was in grave doubt; the
mission was in debt and the issue of slavery had led to the formation
of a separate Southern Baptist Convention. Funds were in crisis. But
despite his inability to engage in any public speaking (due to the lung
complaint) he managed to swing opinion behind expansion rather
than retrenchment.

In November he left his three children with suitable families. A few
days after the painful goodbyes a letter arrived telling him that little
Charlie, aged one year and seven months, had died on 5 August 1845 at
Moulmain. Four years before he and Sarah had watched little Henry
die, also aged one year and seven months. The appalling memories
and the loneliness must have seemed all but overwhelming. But then,
in January 1846, Adoniram found the ideal biographer for Sarah, and
in less than a month he proposed to marry her.

It began when a minister friend gave him a popular book to while
away some time during a delay on a journey. It was by a young woman,
Emily Chubbuck, who wrote under the name of Fanny Forrester. All
her works sparkled with a lively personality. When he found out that
she was a committed Christian, Adoniram was immediately struck
that this might be just the person to write Sarah's memoir. When
he met Emily he found that she was far from superficial. She had
worked her way to success from a pitifully poor background. At the

age of eleven she had been out working in a factory. Of that period she later said, 'My principal recollections during this summer are of noise and filth, bleeding hands and aching feet, and a very sad heart.'[6] Largely self-taught, she had turned to teaching and writing in order to support her needy parents. As 'Fanny Forrester' Emily was highly thought of by literary critics, but she was also intensely religious, having been converted at the age of eight. As a young girl she had been moved to the depths of her being by the account of the deaths of Ann and Maria Judson and had sensed a nagging inward 'call' to missionary work ever since.

Return to Burma with Emily (1846)

Adoniram and Emily met in January, they married in June and left for Burma in July. Friends were dubious as to how the twenty-nine-year-old writer would adapt to the rigours of missionary life but, as with Ann and Sarah, Adoniram had chosen well. Each of his wives was enormously gifted in her own right. Emily confounded all the critics by learning the language in an extraordinarily short time, by cheerfully enduring some of the most miserable conditions even Adoniram had ever experienced and by proving to be an exemplary mother to his surviving children.

When Adoniram (now aged fifty-eight) and Emily arrived back in Moulmain at the end of November 1846, they were not to know that he had only four years left. The mission at Moulmain (in the area under British protection) was prospering, and Adoniram longed that the gospel be taken once more into the territory still controlled by the Burmese king. He set off almost immediately, with Emily and the two remaining little ones, to Rangoon. They managed to hang on there for six months, Judson working on his dictionary and Emily on her memoir of Sarah. Conditions were atrocious and the health of

all the family gave way. The greatest discouragement, however, was the news that the mission board had sent orders for retrenchment; due to lack of funds they were unable to finance the establishment of a mission in Burma proper. Adoniram accepted that the Lord was sovereignly overruling events, but he was bitterly disappointed at the seeming lukewarmness of American Christians. The family was forced to move back to the mission base at Moulmain. In December 1847 a little girl was born, named Emily Frances.

1848 was a happy year: Adoniram and Emily enjoying each of the three little ones, Adoniram superintending the growing mission, Emily fluent enough in Burmese to teach a Bible Class and lead a ladies' prayer meeting. In January 1849 Adoniram completed his dictionary. But in 1849 both Adoniram and Emily were struck down with poor health. By March 1850 Adoniram was told only a sea voyage might save his life. Emily was expecting another baby, and she would not be able to accompany him. She knew that Adoniram was dying, yet could not overrule the doctors who insisted that a voyage held out a slim chance of survival.

Death (12 April 1850)

The ship sailed on 6 April 1850. Adoniram died and was buried at sea just six days later. Ten days after that, Emily gave birth to their son, Charles. He died at birth. Although Adoniram had died only a few hundred miles west of Burma, Emily had to wait four agonizing months before the news got back to Moulmain at the end of August. At first she wanted to continue with mission work in Burma, but ill-health forced her to return to America with the three children in 1851. She then helped Dr Frances Wayland to write his definitive two-volume biography of Adoniram. Three years later, in 1854, she died of tuberculosis.

The legacy

Ann and Adoniram Judson arrived in Burma in 1813. By the time of Adoniram's death in 1850 a strong church had been established among the Karen people. The translation of the Bible, the dictionary, the tracts and catechism—all these had provided a firm foundation for future evangelization.

Today, a very significant number of the minority people groups in Burma are Baptist Christians. Overall, of the total population of 51 million, around 8.9 per cent would profess to be Christian. But the minority peoples are looked down on by the main people group of Burma which is overwhelmingly Buddhist. The central government has declared that to be Burmese is to be Buddhist, and in recent years directives have been issued for the elimination of Christianity. Even in this unpromising context, the church maintains a strong missionary vision.[7]

The vision: 'Nothing is difficult to omnipotence'

Adoniram Judson's vision had not been confined to Burma. He longed for the evangelization of the whole world, and prayed fervently for the churches in America to be mobilized to that end. Wayland noted: 'As Mr Judson believed that this was the work of God, one thing seemed to him just as easy as another. *Nothing is difficult to omnipotence.*'[8] The life ambition of Adoniram Judson was aptly expressed in his parting address to American Christians before his final return to Burma in 1846:

> The world is yet in its infancy; the gracious designs of God are yet hardly developed. Glorious things are spoken of Zion, the city of our God. She is yet to triumph, and become the joy and glory of the whole earth. Blessed be God that we live in these latter times—the latter times of the reign of darkness and

imposture. Great is our privilege, precious our opportunity, to co-operate with the Saviour in the blessed work of enlarging and establishing His kingdom throughout the world ...

Let us not, then, regret the loss of those who have gone before us, and are waiting to welcome us back home, nor shrink from the summons that must call us thither. Let us only resolve to follow them who, through faith and patience, inherit the promises. Let us so employ the remnant of life, and so pass away, that our successors will say of us, as we of our predecessors, 'Blessed are the dead that die in the Lord. They rest from their labours, and their works do follow them.'[9]

Select bibliography

Works used

Chatterjee, Sumil Kumar. *Felix Carey, A Tiger Tamed*. Calcutta, 1991.

Judson, Ann H. *An Account of the American Baptist Mission to the Burman Empire: in a series of letters addressed to a Gentleman in London*. London, 1823.

Judson, Edward. *Adoniram Judson, D.D. His Life and Labours*. London, 1883.

Kendrick, A. C. *The Life and Labours of Mrs Emily C. Judson*. London, 1862.

Knowles, James D. *Memoir of Mrs Ann H. Judson*. London, 1829.

Wayland, Francis. *A Memoir of the Life and Labours of the Rev. Adoniram Judson, D.D.* Two volumes. London, 1853.

Woods, Leonard. *Memoirs of Mrs Harriet Newell, wife of the Rev. S. Newell, American Missionary to India*. London, 1816.

A number of unpublished letters, kept at the Angus Library, Regents College, Oxford. Thanks are expressed to Sue Mills for giving access to these.

Recommended for further reading:

Anderson, Courtney. *To the Golden Shore: The Life of Adoniram Judson.* Judson Press, Valley Forge, USA. 1956, rep. 1987, 530pp. This is a classic missionary biography, telling the drama of Adoniram's life in an unforgettable way.

Hulse, Erroll. *Adoniram Judson and the Missionary Call.* Reformation Today Trust, 1996. 64pp. This is a readable introduction to Judson's life with applications for today.

Notes

Introduction to the 1998 Edition

1. Lydia Maria Child, quoted in *Christianity in America: A Handbook*, Lion Publishing, 1983, p. 192.

2. Three women left America with their husbands in 1812. Harriet, wife of Samuel Newell, died before the end of the year. Samuel and Roxana Nott were forced to leave India due to ill health in 1816.

3. Ann's private journal survived up to October 1813, and Knowles used large sections. After that he quoted liberally from her book *An Account of the American Baptist Mission to the Burman Empire* which was published in 1823. (*Memoir* pp. 134–5).

4. There is a sympathetic section on Moung (Ko) Ing and his ministry in Amherst in Edward Judson's biography of his father, pp. 340–342.

Chapter 1

1. Kenneth Scott Latourette, *A History of Christianity*, 2 vols., New York, 1975, vol. II, p. 1229.

2. Ibid. p. 1230.

3. Iain Murray, *Revival and Revivalism: the Making and Marring of American Evangelicalism, 1750–1858*, Banner of Truth, Edinburgh, 1994, p. 124.

4. Knowles, *Memoir*, and Leonard Woods, *Memoirs of Mrs Harriet Newell*, London, 1816.

5. Hannah More (1745–1833) was a religious writer and philanthropist in England, and a significant figure in the Evangelical Awakening. *Strictures on Female Education* was a book which aimed to point women away from a trivial and worldly way of life.

Chapter 2

1. Woods, *Harriet Newell*, p. 69.

Chapter 3

1. See Appendix III for a biographical sketch of Adoniram Judson.
2. Woods, *Harriet Newell*, p. 77.
3. Ibid. p. 61.
4. E. Judson, *Adoniram Judson*, pp. 20–21.

Chapter 4

1. Quoted in Courtney Anderson, *To The Golden Shore: The Life of Adoniram Judson*, Judson Press, Valley Forge, 1956, rep. 1987, p. 112.

Chapter 5

1. John Bowker, ed., *The Oxford Dictionary of World Religions*, OUP, Oxford, 1997, p. 486.
2. Timothy George, *Faithful Witness: The Life and Mission of William Carey*, IVP, Leicester, 1991, p. 126.
3. The East India Company was given a charter by Queen Elizabeth I in 1600, and traded at first in the Moluccas. From about 1610 it established bases on the Indian mainland, and through the eighteenth century built up British trading interests. From 1773 onwards authority in India was gradually transferred to the British government, a process only completed in 1858.
4. The position of the British Baptists was very vulnerable until after 1813, when the East India Company's Charter was revised. Carey and his colleagues had only managed to establish themselves because Serampore was in Danish-controlled

territory—except from 1801–2 and 1808–15, when it came under British control (Brian Stanley, *History of the Baptist Missionary Society*, T. & T. Clark, Edinburgh, 1992, p. 54).

5. Frances Wayland, *A Memoir of the Life and Labours of the Rev. Adoniram Judson, D.D.*, 2 vols, London, 1853, vol. 1, pp. 79–80. Letter written 7 September 1812.

6. Ibid. p. 81. Letter written from Isle of France, Port Louis, 14 February 1813.

7. E. Judson, *Adoniram Judson*, pp. 42–3.

Chapter 6

1. It should be noted that while the inhabitants of New England did not witness such scenes of brutality, the suffering of slaves in the southern states of America was just as appalling.

Chapter 7

1. Anderson, *Golden Shore*, pp. 139–40.

2. Woods, *Harriet Newell*, p. 166.

3. E. Judson, *Adoniram Judson*, pp. 51–2.

4. Ibid. p.76.

5. Wayland, *Adoniram Judson*, vol. 1, note, p. 123.

6. See chapter 20, note 2.

Chapter 8

1. Anderson, *Golden Shore*, p. 176.

2. Sumil Kumar Chatterjee, *Felix Carey: A Tiger Tamed*, Calcutta, 1991. This is a sympathetic treatment of Felix Carey's brief and rather sad life. His diplomatic work was a disaster. At the beginning of 1815 he remarried; his third wife was a French girl, fifteen years old. She was left alone in a large house in Rangoon, while Felix travelled around the eastern part of India seeking alternative employment. It is not clear whether she had any contact with the Judsons, and she died some time before 1822, when Felix married for the fourth time. By then he had returned to Serampore, to work once more in the mission printing department. He died

in 1822 aged thirty-six. Felix was an extremely gifted linguist, and translated a number of valuable works into Bengali and other languages.

3. Ann Judson, *An Account of the American Baptist Mission to the Burman Empire*, London, 1823. p. 31.

4. Ibid. pp. 27–8.

5. The *Memoir*, p. 140 incorrectly gives the date for Ann's trip to Madras as 1814. Ann's letter of 26 September 1815 (143–4) indicates that the trip was made in that year.

Chapter 9

1. E. Judson, *Adoniram Judson*, pp. 96–7.

2. Quoted in Anderson, *Golden Shore*, p. 192.

Chapter 10

1. Ann Judson, *Account*, pp. 118–19.

Chapter 11

1. Ann Judson, *Account*, pp. 156–7.

2. The Burmese used the following titles: Moung for a young man, Oo for an older man, Men for a girl, Mah for a young woman and May for an old woman.

Chapter 12

1. Portion of unpublished letter, held in the Angus Library.

2. The Colmans built a house and started a mission in a village outside Chittagong. James Colman died in July 1822. Mrs Colman then worked as a teacher in Bengal, before marrying an English Baptist missionary.

Chapter 13

1. Wayland, *Adoniram Judson*, vol. 1, p. 231.

2. Roy Porter, *The Greatest Benefit to Mankind: A Medical History of Humanity from Antiquity to the Present*, Harper-Collins, London, 1997, p. 674. Senna was a plant-based purgative. Blue pills were popular through the early nineteenth

century. They contained mercury, were prescribed for all manner of ailments and probably did more harm than good (see chapter 15).

3. Wayland, *Adoniram Judson*, vol. 1, p. 240.

Chapter 14

1. Unpublished letter, held in the Angus Library.
2. Unpublished letter, held in the Angus Library.
3. These two letters are held in the Angus Library. They were published in an article in the *Baptist Quarterly*, new series, vol. 5. 1930–1931, pp. 372–5, entitled 'Ann Hasseltine Judson's Letters'

Chapter 15

1. Ann Judson, *Account,* pp. v–vi.
2. Porter, *Greatest Benefit*, p. 266.
3. Ibid. p. 314.
4. Ibid. p. 266.
5. Hendrick, Joan D., *Harriet Beecher Stowe: A Life,* OUP, Oxford, 1994, p. 175.
6. Ann Judson, *Account* (supplement, letter 15), pp. 327–8.
7. Wayland, *Adoniram Judson*, vol. 1, p. 242.

Chapter 16

1. E. Judson, *Adoniram Judson,* p. 195.
2. Wayland, *Adoniram Judson*, vol. 1, p. 250.
3. Ann Judson, *Account,* supplement, p. 328.
4. Ibid. pp. 328–9.
5. Ibid. (letter 16), pp. 330–33.
6. Ibid. p. 333.

Chapter 17

1. Ann Judson, *Account*, supplement, p. 334.

Chapter 18

1. Her account of the captivity prepared for Elnathan Judson was published by Knowles in the *Memoir*, pp. 281–324. Portions of this account form the basis for chapters 18–21.
2. Wayland, *Adoniram Judson*, vol. 1, p. 303.
3. Ibid. pp. 299–230.

Chapter 19

1. E. Judson, *Adoniram Judson*, p. 268.
2. Ibid. pp. 268–71.

Chapter 20

1. Wayland, *Adoniram Judson*, vol. 1, p. 312.
2. 'The one eighteenth-century improvement in practical medicine which decisively saved lives was the introduction first of inoculation and then of vaccination against smallpox.' Up to that time, in bad years smallpox may have been responsible for a tenth of all deaths in Europe. Inoculation (using a mild dose of smallpox) was common from early in the eighteenth century. Edward Jenner first used a cowpox inoculation to protect against smallpox in 1796 (Porter, *Greatest Benefit*, pp. 274–6).
3. A preparation containing opium.

Chapter 21

1. Unpublished letter, to Mrs Deakin, written from Rangoon, 12 May 1826. Held in the Angus Library.
2. Wayland, *Adoniram Judson*, vol. 1, pp. 316–17.
3. Knowles notes that Price wished to use his influence at court to promote the gospel, and wrote that Price 'was fully persuaded, that his situation would enable him to serve the cause of the Redeemer with great success' (357–8). He was employed both as a court doctor, but also as a tutor to sons of officials. He died in 1828.
4. The *Memoir*, p. 320, refers to the month of March, but the chronology prepared

by Adoniram Judson makes it clear that this journey took place on 21 February (Judson, E., *Adoniram Judson*, p. 564).

5. Wayland, *Adoniram Judson*, vol. 1, pp. 318–20.

6. Ibid. pp. 320–21

Chapter 22

1. Unpublished letter, undated. Held in the Angus Library.

2. Unpublished letter, written from Rangoon, 12 May 1826, Angus Library.

Chapter 23

1. E. Judson, *Adoniram Judson*, pp. 374–5.

2. Wayland, *Adoniram Judson*, vol. 2, p. 329.

3. Letter written 20 January 1847, A. C. Kendrick, *The Life and Letters of Mrs Emily C. Judson*, London, 1862, p. 237.

Appendix I

1. E. Judson, *Adoniram Judson*, p. 73.

2. Kendrick, *Emily Judson*, p. 19.

3. E. Judson, *Adoniram Judson*, p. 483.

Appendix II

1. Written in Boston, on 19 November 1822, Knowles, *Memoir*, pp. 396–400.

Appendix III

1. The value of this work is debated. Wayland dismissed the work done by Chater and Carey as inaccurate. Wayland, *Adoniram Judson*, vol.1, p. 123.

2. Ibid. vol. 2.p. 137.

3. Ibid. vol. 2. p. 138.

4. At this time when missionaries went to Asia, it was likely to be 'for life'. When children reached the age of eight or so, they were usually sent back to America and settled with friends or family. This was so that they could get schooling,

and also because of the risks of tropical sickness. Parents and children did not know whether they would ever see one another again. Children would be sent home when some suitable escort was going back. The return trip of Adoniram and Sarah proved to be just such an opportunity to take the three older children. The three younger children were going to be living in Burma with their parents for a few more years, and it was evidently thought inadvisable to expose them needlessly to the risks of the long sea voyage.

5. Wayland, *Adoniram Judson,* vol. 2, p. 166.

6. Kendrick, *Emily Judson,* p. 16.

7. Jason Mandryk, *Operation World,* Seventh Edition, Biblica Publishing, 2010, p. 613.

8. Wayland, *Adoniram Judson,* vol. 1, p. 163.

9. E. Judson, *Adoniram Judson,* p. 491.